Mysteries around UFOs and Aliens

Vikas Khatri

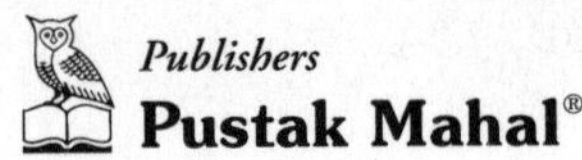

Administrative office and sale centre
J-3/16 , Daryaganj, New Delhi-110002
☎ 23276539, 23272783, 23272784 • *Fax:* 011-23260518
E-mail: info@pustakmahal.com • *Website:* www.pustakmahal.com

Branches
Bengaluru: ☎ 080-22234025 • *Telefax:* 080-22240209
E-mail: pustak@airtelmail.in • pustak@sancharnet.in
Mumbai: ☎ 022-22010941, 022-22053387
E-mail: rapidex@bom5.vsnl.net.in
Patna: ☎ 0612-3294193 • *Telefax:* 0612-2302719
E-mail: rapidexptn@rediffmail.com

ISBN 978-81-223-0944-7

Edition: 2014

Printed at : **Radha Offset, Delhi**

Contents

Introduction

The letters **UFO** stands for 'Unidentified Flying Object'. If we know what they were, they would be IFOs – 'Identified Flying Objects. Through the centuries, people have observed unusual object's in the sky. From about 1950, these stories have received much publicity in newspapers. Many were hoaxes. Many turned out to be distant stars or planets. However, there have always been quite a number of unsolved mysteries.

Ufologists are people who study UFOs. The UFOs are most often seen at night. The brightest planet, Venus, is very often mistaken for UFO. The UFO sightings at close quarters are now referred to as close encounters. A close encounter of the first kind is sighting of a UFO, which is fairly close. There is no contact with the UFO and it does not land. In a close encounter of the second kind, there are physical traces of the UFO as well as a sighting. For example, people have reported the UFOs causing their car engines and lights to fail. The most exciting and amazing UFO sighting is a close encounter of the third kind, for living creatures are seen in or near the UFO. Some of them seem to be *grotesque little goblins* whereas others are creatures like human beings, intelligent with peculiar skin and clothing.

Can the UFOs really be spacecrafts from other world? If so, where do they come from, and how do they get here? Some Ufologists think that they may be timetravel machines and, perhaps, not material in the sense we understand it. This would explain why there are so many reports of the UFOs, which suddenly disappeared in thin air. It is also possible that the UFOs come from other universes completely unknown to us. It would be a dramatic solution to the puzzles and problems of the UFOs.

1. George Adamski

The first and still the most famous of the early contactees. Born in 1891, he was 62 when he published his story in 1953 of alleged contactee meetings with aliens from another world. In his book, *Flying Saucers Have Landed,* he revealed that he had been sighting the UFOs since 1946, and he had met his first alien at 12.30 in the afternoon on Thursday, the 20, November 1952, in the California desert, 16 km from Desert Center, towards Arizona.

He and the alien apparently communicated in a combination of sign language and telepathy. Adamski referred to himself as professor George Adamski. How he acquired the title of 'Professor' is not clear. Adamski also made much of his connection with Mount Palomar, the world's largest telescope, though, in fact, his real connection to this was that he served hamburgers in a tourist café on the slopes, a detail which he later clarified in his books. Adamski's alien indicated that he came from Venus, which he described as being Earth's sister planet. However, subsequent years have revealed that Venus is far from compatible with Earth.

During his conversations Adamski was told that the humanoid form was universal and it was also indicated that aliens were abducting human beings. On this point, it is unclear whether the alien meant, 'abduction' in the sense of this encyclopedia. He may have meant permanently kidnapping them.

Adamski later went on to travel in flying saucers throughout the solar system meeting Martians, Saturnians and Jovians. Adamski has many supporters to the present day though modern UFO researchers have called many of his claims into question. The most obvious problem is that science has overtaken many of his claims. We know Venus will not support humanoid life; so we now know that Adamski could not have stepped on to the surface of the gas giant planets, if they have surfaces!

2. Hessdalen Project

Between 1981 and 1985, Project Hessdalen in Scandinavia became the centre of a prolonged study of the UFOs.

The first reports came from the Norwegian valley of Hessdalen, south-west of Trondheim. Hundreds of witnesses described variously shaped illuminated 'objects,' including fast and slow-moving lights, of Christmas tree shapes, and so on.

Over a period of years, an investigative team 'staked out' the valley and took many photographs and made films of the lights. In June 1983, this stimulated the formation of Project

Hessdalen formed between UFO Norway, UFO Sweden, Finnish Ufological groups and the Society for Psycho Bio-Physics.

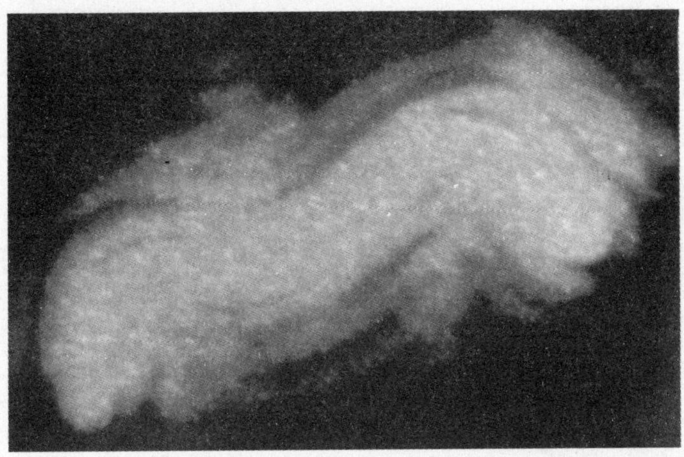

Leif Havik, Odd-Gunnar Roed, Hakan Ekstrand, Jan Fjellander and Erling Strand directed the project. A great deal of equipments was used during the observations, including Atlas 2,000 radar, seismographs, magnetometers, spectrum analysers, infrared viewers, geiger counters and all forms of camera devices.

There was some indication that the lights were interactive with the investigators, and the suggestion has been made that they were some forms of intelligence though such conclusions are highly speculative at this time.

What Project Hessdalen serves to confirm without doubt is that there is a UFO phenomenon, i.e. a phenomenon of genuinely unexplained events. It also showed that cooperation between researchers could produce impressive results when there was a significant duration of a sighting involved.

3. Kenneth Arnold's Historic Sightings

Idaho businessman, Kenneth Arnold, was an experienced pilot. On June 24, 1947, he was flying east across the Cascade Mountain from Chehalis to Yakima, Washington. He was enticed by the offer of $5000 reward to spend an hour or so searching for a Marine Corps C-46 transport aircraft that had recently come down near Mount Rainier with 32 men on board. Arnold's aircraft was specially designed for working in mountainous terrain. He took off from Chehalis airport at 2:00 p.m.

Kenneth Arnold was in the midst of his search at an altitude of about 2750 m above the town of Mineral (about 40 km south-west of the peak of Mount Rainier). As he was making a 180° turn, 'a tremendously bright flash lit up the surfaces of his aircraft. Arnold looked for the source of the flash, but the only other plane in the vicinity was a Douglas DC-4 airliner. Arnold then figured he had seen a flash of sunlight off his wings of a close-flying fighter; he speculated that he had been buzzed by a P-51 Mustang, the most powerful fighter then in common service with the USAF.

Before he had time to look for a fast-moving Mustang, however, Arnold saw another flash and where it came from! "I observed," he reported, "far to my left and to the north, a formation of very bright objects coming from the vicinity of Mount Baker, flying very close to the mountain tops and travelling at a tremendous speed." They were moving almost directly across Arnold's own flightpath, which made it easy to calculate their speed. Arnold was amazed to discover that the nine crafts were travelling at over 2750 km/h, well beyond the capability of any conventional aircraft at the time. What made this phenomenal speed all the more extraordinary was the way the craft were flying.

Arnold said later: "They didn't fly like any aircraft I had seen before......they flew in a definite formation, but erratically......like speed boats on rough water or similar to the tail of a Chinese kite that l once saw blowing in the wind........They fluttered and sailed, tipping their wings alternately and emitting very bright blue-white flashes from their surfaces."

Arnold decided to abandon his search for the missing C-46 and make for Yakima to report what he had seen. Landing there at about 4:00 p.m, he told his story to an airline manger and discussed it with other professional fliers, before taking off once more for Pendleton, Oregon. The news flew ahead of him. Among the crowd to greet him was a reporter, Bill Becquette, from the *East Oregonian* newspaper. Arnold described the craft he had seen as flying "like a saucer would if you skipped it across the water." From these words came the term 'flying saucers'. By now, Arnold was sure that he had seen a flight of guided missiles, 'robotly controlled'. He concluded that the government had chosen this way to announce the discovery of 'a new principle of flight'.

Becquette put the story on the Associated Press wire. For three days at Pendleton, Arnold was beseiged with enquiries. Finally, exhausted and unable to work, Arnold flew 320 km across the state line to his home in Boise, ldaho. Shortly after arriving there, Arnold had a telephone call from Dave Johnson, aviation editor of the *ldaho Statesman* newspaper.

The conversation changed everything for Arnold: "I am sure he was in a position to know........that it was not a new military- guided missile and.......if what I had seen was true, it did not belong to the good old USA. It was then that I really began to wonder."

4. Secret Talks in Greece

Eminent Greek scientist, Paul Santorini, stunned members of his country's astronauticals, society in February 1967 when he announced that there was 'a world blanket of secrecy' about UFO activities, because the authorities did not want to admit the existence of forces against which our planet, Earth had 'no possibility of defence'.

Professor Santorini, then over 70 and the most respected scientist in Greece, revealed that in 1947, the Greek army had called him in to lead a team of engineers to investigate what were thought to be Russian missiles flying over the country.

"We soon established that they were not missiles," he said. "But before we could do any more, the army, after conferring with foreign officials, ordered the investigation stopped. Foreign scientists flew to Greece for secret talks with me."

Professor Santorini added that he had no doubt aliens were "visiting Earth to collect plant and animal specimens", but he would not guess why.

5. They Liked Lavender Plants

On July 1, 1965, in the early hours of the morning, a French farmer, Maurice Masse, at Valensole was attracted to the sight of a landed object in his lavender field by a strange high-pitched sound.

The object was shaped like an egg with a cupola on top and was approximately 5 m wide. It was standing on six legs in a manner reminiscent of a spider, according to the witness. The door of the object was open and within it, Masse could see two seats.

Near the object were what Masse took to be two young boys apparently taking lavender plants. They turned out to be entities from the object about one-and-half metre tall and clad in green ski suits. When they noticed Masse approaching, one of them levelled a rod towards him, which immobilised him.

On further examination, the entities appeared to have large bald heads, big slanting eyes, pronounced chins and small lipless mouths. They made guttural sounds.

This style of entity is often recounted by Americans under hypnosis in most fearful terms. But Masse's conscious recall remembers them as good-natured beings, who brought a sense of peace to him. It is interesting that many American cases involving these entities combine fear with a great desire to be with the creatures.

While Masse was still immobilised, the entities returned to their craft and took off, with the landing legs retracting. After some considerable time, Masse was able to move. Four days after the event occurred, he fell into a deep sleep and members of his family fought to wake him up. They believed that otherwise he would have slept for a very extended period. Usually, Masse slept only five or six hours a night, but for months after the event, he needed at least twelve-hours sleep.

The most remarkable of the ground traces was that no lavender plants would grow at the landing site for ten years.

6. UFO Waves

Though it may sound bizarre, grotesque dwarflike aliens in diving suits were reported in Quaroble, France, on September 10, 1954. A week later, a French farmer was bicycling near the town of Cenon when he suddenly started to itch all over.

When he stopped alongside the road and dismounted, he became immobilised at the sight of a 'machine' ahead of him. A small diving suit-clad creature approached, uttered strange sounds, and touched the farmer's shoulder. It then returned to the object and disappeared inside. The UFO glowed green, as it rose into the air and sped away.

Some ten days later, four French children were playing in their father's barn. Hearing the dog bark, the eldest boy went out to investigate and confronted a rectangular creature that, he said, resembled a 'sugar cube.' Throwing pebbles and shooting a toy arrow at the ET, the boy was pushed to the ground by an invisible force. As he scrambled away, he saw the creature waddle off toward the meadow. Running back to the house, the children saw a glowing red object hovering over the meadow. The next day, investigators discovered a circle of burnt grass.

A couple of weeks after that, another Frenchman reported an encounter with a 1.2 m tall creature in what, again, resembled a diving suit. The creature shuffled along the road before disappearing into the adjacent trees. The next days, three children saw another 1.2 m tall creature emerge from a 'shiny machine.' Later describing the creature as a 'ghost' with a hairy face and big eyes, dressed in something akin to a priest's cassock, the children said the creature spoke words they didn't understand.

The following day, three men from Bordeaux were driving near Royan on the Atlantic coast of France when they observed a craft hovering about 10 m above the ground. Getting out of their car to investigate, they came upon 1.2 m tall creatures seemingly making repairs under a craft.

According to the experts, the UFO reports come in waves. There was a rush of sighting throughout the western hemisphere as well as in Australia and Asia from 1957 to 1958, and in South America from 1977 to 1978. But out of all the UFO waves, the 1954 French waves were the most intense.

7. The Landing at Socorro

About six hours after Wilcox's bizarre encounter in New York state, another close encounter took place in New Mexico. On April 24, 1964 at roughly 5:45 p.m., local time patrolman, Lonnie Zamora, on duty in the Socorro police cruiser, gave chase to a speeding black Chevrolet. The pursuit continued south out of town. At that time, Zamora heard a brief roar and saw a flame in the sky to his right. He knew that there was a shack containing dynamite in the vicinity; he thought it had blown up. He abandoned his chase and swung off the highway onto a dirty road that led over a ridge and past the shack. The flame, blue and orange, smokeless, long and narrow — was now descending towards the ground.

Zamora drove slowly down the other side of the ridge. The noise had stopped and the flame had vanished. He suddenly noticed 'a shiny type of object to the south' between 90-180 m off the road and below him in a gully. "It looked," Zamora

told FBI agent, J. Arthur Byrnes Jr, later the same day, "like a car turned upside down, standing on (its) radiator or trunk."

Next to the object were 'two people in white coveralls. One of them turned and looked straight at my car. They seemed startled and wanted to quickly jump somewhat. They seemed 'normal, in shape, but possibly, they were small adults or large kids.' Zamora radioed Sgt. Sam Chavez in Socorro. He approached on foot to within 30 m of the object. He saw it was oval and smooth, with no windows or doors, on girder-like legs, and noted red insignia on its side, about 0.75 m wide. Then the roar began again, of low frequency at

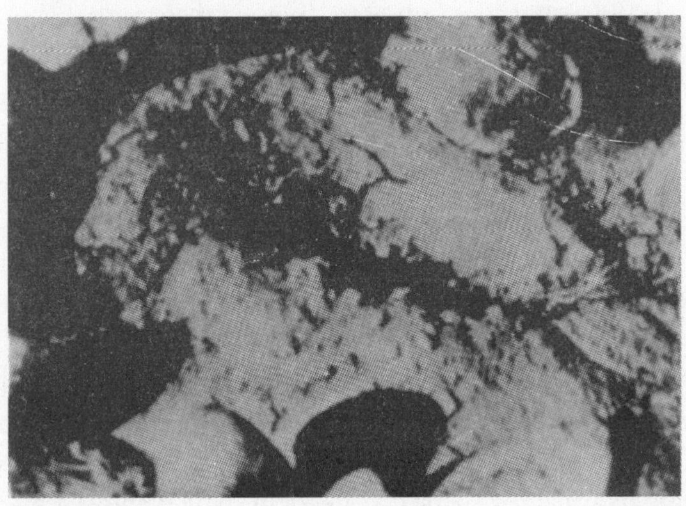

first, rising rapidly and getting 'very loud'. The object emitted flame and kicked up dust. There was no sign of the 'persons' he had seen before.

Zamora thought the thing might explode, and ran back beyond his car to the top of the ridge. The roar stopped, and he looked back to see the UFO going away from him in a south-west direction. It was possibly 3-4.5 m above the ground, and it cleared the dynamite shack by about a metre. The UFO, now travelling very fast but no longer emitting either noise or flame, rose up and sped away. It 'just cleared' a mountain in the distance and disappeared.

8. UFO Crash - Roswell, New Mexico

About 9:50 p.m. on July 8, 1947, Roswell, hardware dealer, Dan Wilmot and his wife were sitting on their front step when they saw a 'big glowing object' travelling at great speed through the sky out of the south-east. It was, they said, like "two inverted saucers faced mouth to mouth".

The Foster Ranch, 'Mac' Brazel's rough, isolated spread, lay 48 km from Corona and 120 km northwest of Roswell. It was a stormy night of July 2nd, 1947. Brazel thought he heard an explosion over the sound of thunder. The next day, checking his sheep, Brazel came across some wreckage that spread in a 350 m trail across his land, pointing due west towards Socorro, a town on the Rio Grande, about 160 kilometres away. The debris was a 'metallic, foil-like substance which was very thin, pliable and tough. He could not crease it or give it a permanent bend. On it was some obscure markings. Some fragments had a 'tape-like material' attached to them, which showed a floral pattern when held up to the light. Soon, in Corona, he heard, for the first time about the rash of the UFO sightings in the area. Wondering if the wreckage on his land was connected, he told the US Army at Roswell of his find. Major Jesse Marcel and a Counter-Intelligence Corps agent went with him to inspect the debris.

The next day troops descended on the sight, keeping everyone off the land until they had cleared it. Marcel stated in 1978 that the wreckage he saw was like 'nothing made on Earth'. It resisted prolonged attack by blowtorch and an 8 kg. sledgehammer. Despite its thinness and, if crumpled, it slowly reverted to its original form.

Also on July 8, civil engineer, Grady L. Barnett of Socorro, was working in the desert about 4.8 km from where the debris was scattered. Then he saw what he thought might be a crashed aircraft. He found 'some sort of metallic, disk-shaped object'; about 9 m in diameter, split open. Inside it, and beside it on the ground, were a number of bodies. They were small, hairless humanoids with large heads, wearing gray, one-piece suits without fasteners. Barnett was soon joined by a group of archaeology students. Soon, a US Army jeep roared up. The officer on board declared the area off

limits and under military control. The area was cordoned off, the civilians were told to leave, and to say nothing of what they have seen. Shortly after, the troops began to move in. The crashed disk had been detected from the air.

The same day a statement printed in the *Roswell Daily Record,* announced that a flying disc had been found and recovered from a ranch, 120 km from Roswell. Later that day, the army called two press conferences, proclaiming that the debris found on Brazel's ranch was the remains of a weather balloon. Reporters saw and photographed it.

There is considerable testimony that secret cargos were flown under heavy guard from Roswell to Fort Worth, Texas and Wright Field (now Wright-Patterson AFB) at Dayton and Ohio, over the next few days.

9. An Early Artistic Classic

The Gorman 'dogfight,' as it is called, lasted for 27 minutes and involved Lt. George F. Gorman of the North Dakota Air National Guard and a UFO. It happened over Fargo, North Dakota, on the night of October 1, 1948. Indeed, it is one of the early classics of the genre.

Gorman, who had been on a cross-country flight with his squadron, had decided to stay up after the other planes had landed and log some more night-flying time. At about 9 p.m, he was preparing to land when the control tower informed him of another craft –a Piper Cub—in the vicinity. Gorman could see this plane clearly below him, but then what appeared to be was the taillight of the another plane flashed by him on the right. When the tower informed him that they knew of no other plane in the vicinity, Gorman decided to investigate. He pulled his F-51 up and towards the moving light. When he was within about 1,000 m of it, he could see the object clearly:

It was about 15-20 cm in diameter, clear white and completely round without fuzz at the edges. It was blinking on and off. Gorman cut sharply towards the light, which again was coming straight at him. Just when collision seemed unavoidable, the UFO streaked straight up in a steep climb and disappeared. When Gorman tried to pursue the object, his plane went into a power stall at about 4,200 m, and he did not see the object again. The total chase had lasted from 9 to 9:27 p.m.

Gorman was so distraught by his encounter that he had trouble landing his plane. He said he had noticed no sound, odour or exhaust trail from the UFO and no deviation on his instruments.

Corroboration of the incident was provided by the two traffic controllers on duty, Lloyd D. Jensen and H. E. Johnson. They saw the strange light at the same time they saw the Pipe Cub. They described it in very much the same term as Gorman— "a round light, perfectly formed, with no fuzzy edges or rays leaving its body." Both of them noted its apparent high rate of speed. Two further witnesses— the pilot of the Piper Cub and his passenger— not only saw the swiftly moving light but also observed the object and Gorman's plane in pursuit.

Gorman stated that he was convinced that the UFO demonstrated "thought" in its manoeuvers and that he was chasing an extraordinary "guided craft" of some kind. No satisfactory conventional explanation for the Gorman "dogfight" has ever been offered.

10. UFO and Bigfoot

One night in February 1974, the sounds outside her home startled a Pennsylvanian woman. Not taking any chances, she went to the front door armed with a gun and cautiously stepped out onto the porch. Suddenly, she was confronted by a flesh-and-blood bigfoot-like creature, two metres away. When she shot the gun, aiming for his middle, she was astonished to see it disappear in a burst of light.

Having heard the shot, the woman's son-in-law rushed to her aid. Once outside, he saw other bigfoot creatures at the edge of the nearby woods. Hovering overhead was a bright red flashing light.

There have been a number of cases in which both the UFOs and the Bigfoot have been sighted at the same time and in the same area. Another case involving the humanoid creatures and the UFOs took place on a farm near Gettysburg, Pennsylvania. A twenty-two-year-old farmer's son named Stephen went to investigate a large, bright red luminous ball sighted one night in October 1973. He and the two ten-year-old boys, who accompanied him saw the object hovering close to the ground. Nearby, there were two tall, apelike creatures with green glowing eyes and long, dark hair. When they began to approach the threesome, Stephen fired a shot over their heads. When the creatures continued moving forward, Stephen fired three more times, hitting the largest creature. The UFO suddenly disappeared, and the hairy creatures turned around and walked into the woods.

11. Alien Pancakes

Joe Simonton, a master plumber of Eagle River, Wisconsiin, received four 'pancakes' from the hands of one of the occupants of a UFO that hovered over his yard. On April 18, 1961, Simonton tells of hearing a sound, like "knobby tyres on a wet pavement." Then he saw a silvery object like "two wash bowls turned face to face" just a few centimetres off the ground.

When he approached, a 2 m high hatch opened and he saw three "men" inside. They appeared young and about 1.5 m tall with dark hair and hairless dark faces. One of them handed Simonton a silver-coloured jug with two handles and indicated with a motion that he wanted water. Simonton filled the jug

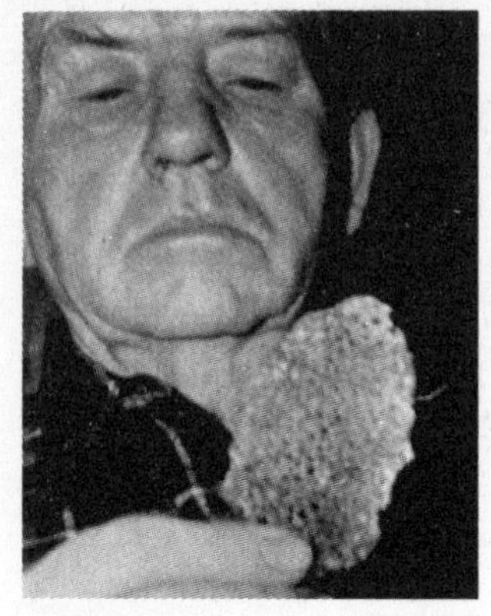

and handed it back. He then saw a man "cooking" on some kind of flameless stove. Seeing a stack of small, perforated cookie like objects next to the "griddle," Simonton motioned that he wanted one. An occupant picked up four of the "pancakes" and gave them to Simonton. Then the UFO rook off at a 45-degreee angle, creating a great rush of wind that bowed over the pine trees nearby. Simonton ate one of the cookies and said later that it "tasted like cardboard." He kept a second one and gave the remaining two to various UFO investigation committees. The group from Northwestern University apparently said that the cookie, they had checked, contained "flour, sugar and grease."

12. They Came for Hair Sample

Carlos Alberto Diaz, a 28-year-old waiter in the town of Ingeiero White, Argentina, was found lying by the side of the road about 7 a.m. on January 5, 1975. His scalp was exposed in spots where tufts of hair were missing. He was driven some 50 km to a hospital in Buenos Aires (about 560 km from his hometown), and there Diaz claimed that his hair had been forcibly removed by three humanoids with rubbery "moss green" skin and stumpy arms with suckers. Forty-six doctors and specialists and several police investigators questioned and examined Diaz, who quietly and believably adhered to his story of abduction.

He stated that he had left work in the predawn that morning. On his walk home, he was crossing a deserted railroad yard when he saw a very bright but "broken" beam of light, which he took for lightning, which temporarily blinded him. When his sight returned, he found himself paralysed, and heard a persistent "hum" in the air. Suddenly, he felt himself being "*drawn and absorbed upward*" by what he described as the "windy humming of the beam." Then he fainted.

He awoke inside a smooth, shining unfurnished "sphere" about 2.5 m wide and 3 m high. Three entities "slid" into the room and started pressing their peculiar arms against his long hair, somehow "sucking up" whole tufts of it at a time but without causing any pain. The heads of these beings were half the size of ours and totally hairless; their moss-green faces were featureless, lacking eyes, nose, mouth and ears. They were about 1.7 m tall and had slim bodies covered with soft, pale, cream-coloured "rubber." While they "extracted" clumps of Diaz's hair, they jumped up and down gleefully. After working on his head, they started to remove tufts of hair from his chest. Diaz fainted again.

Some hours later, Diaz found himself stretched out on the grass in the bright morning sunlight. The bag he had been carrying was lying next to him. Glancing at his watch, he saw that it had stopped at 3:50 a.m., whereas it was now obviously much later. He felt nauseous and began to vomit. At that point, a motorist noticed him and came to his aid.

The medical examinations established that Diaz's head and chest hair had indeed been removed. Some of it seemed to have been "sheared off," but quite a bit had been extracted by the roots, leaving the surrounding capillary tissues completely clean. How this could have been done is uncertain. One theory is that the "beings" created enough suction to "dilate" the capillary bulbs around the roots so that the individual hair came out smoothly. The medical team found nothing wrong with Diaz except the missing hair and the nausea, which persisted for several days.

13. Intelligent Behaviour of UFO

At 10:55 on the night of August 13, 1956, a radar operator at the American-leased Royal Air Force (RAF) Bentwaters base near Ipswich, England picked up a fast-moving target. It appeared when it was just 50 km to the east, travelling at 3,200 to 6,400 km/h. It was heading in from the sea.

A tower operator described the object as "blurred out by its high speed," as it passed directly over the base. Alerted by ground control, an American pilot saw a fuzzy light flash between his aircraft and the ground.

Bentwaters' controller notified the Americans at the RAF's Lakenheath base, where the UFO seemed headed. Shortly afterwards, Lakenheath radar recorded objects travelling at an incredible speed, stopping suddenly, and instantaneously changing course. Ground observers sighted two white lights that came together and disappeared. Officials hesitantly notified the RAF.

The RAF's chief controller dispatched a fighter plane towards the UFO. As the aircraft closed in, however, the UFO suddenly and mysteriously appeared behind the plane. Witnesses said the UFO seemed to flip over as it moved behind the RAF fighter, which then attempted to get behind the UFO.

According to Arizona University atmospheric physicist, James McDonald, "the apparently rational, intelligent behaviour of the UFO suggests a mechanical device of unknown origin as the most probable explanation."

The United States Air Force Condon Report on UFOs described the sighting as one of "the most puzzling and unusual cases" ever to emerge.

14. Were the Early UFOs Manmade?

Some theorists have long sought an earthly explanation for the elusive UFO. The similarities between the advent of the modern flying saucer in the summer of 1947, and the subsequent advances in both Soviet and Western aerospace technology, they argue, are simply too striking for coincidence.

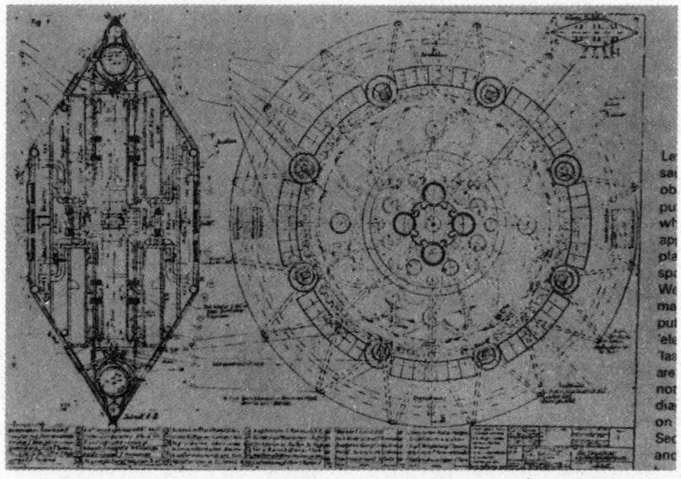

In fact, scattered sources indicate that Hitler's *Luftsaffe*, which deployed the world's first jet fighter, was hard at work developing a range of superscript aerial weaponry during the closing days of World War II. According to a report issued on December 13, 1944, by Marshall Yarrow, a *Reuters* correspondent, "the Germans have produced a 'secret' weapon in keeping with the Christmas season." The new device, which is an air defence weapon, resembles the glass balls that adorn Christmas trees. They have been seen hanging in the air over German territory, sometimes singly, sometimes in clusters. They are silver coloured and are apparently transparent."

Were the flying Christmas balls the 'Foo Fighter' of World War II fame, or had Nazi engineers developed something even more sophisticated? Italian author Renato Velasco alleges that the Germans produced a low-profile, disk-shaped flying machine they dubbed the *Feuerball*, or 'Fire Ball,' used both as an antiradar device and psychological warfare weapon against the Allied forces.

An improved version, the *Kugelbitz*, or "Ball Lightning" fighter, replaced the earlier gas turbine engine of the *Feuerball* with one employing jet propulsion. According to Velasco, the *Kugelblitz* was the first aircraft capable of "jet lift," vertical takeoff and landing. Its designer was Rudolph Scriever, and it was reportedly manufactured at the BMW plant near Prague in 1944. The craft was first flown in February 1945, over the vast underground research complex of Kahla, Thuringia, Germany.

It was also in this same area of the Harz Mountains that Hitler reportedly intended making his last stand, fortified by the awesome array of new "secret weapons," which *Luftwaffe* commander Goering had been repeatedly promising.

Time ran out for the secret Nazi armoury. But if the Soviets or some other power managed to capture flying disk technology, it might have led to experimentation and development of something that gave rise to the frequent reports of early UFOs, starting in 1947.

15. Even Emergency Generator Failed

The coastal fort of Itaipu in Brazil is situated at Sao Vicente, close to the port of Santos in the state of Sao Paulo. To the two sentries patrolling the gun emplacements in the small hours of 4 November 1957, everything seemed quiet. Nothing warned them that within a few minutes, they were to be put through a nightmarish ordeal that still lacks an explanation.

At 2 a.m., the sentries spotted a 'bright star' that suddenly appeared above the horizon over the Atlantic. It grew larger and the soldiers realised that it was approaching them at high speed. This glowing object astonished them, which they thought, was an aeroplane, but they gave no thought to sounding the alarm.

In a few seconds the UFO, travelling silently, reached a point high above the fort and halted. Then it floated down until it had stopped motionless some 50 metres above the highest gun turret, bathing the ground between the turrets with an eerie circular. It was, in the soldiers' words, about the size of a 'big Douglas' (meaning, presumably, a Douglas DC-6). The sentries could now hear a gentle humming noise that seemed to be associated with it.

Without warning, a wave of searing heat suddenly engulfed the men. Fire seemed to be burning all over their uniforms, while the humming intensified.

One sentry staggered, dazed, and then fell unconscious to the ground. His comrade managed to stumble into a relatively sheltered spot beneath one of the guns. But once there his mind seemed to give way, and he was seized by blood-curdling screams.

His terrible cries awakened the rest of the garrison, but within seconds, the power supply was cut off, lights went out and equipment failed. An officer tried to start the emergency generator, but that too failed. Meanwhile, the horrifying screams continued and confusion tuned to panic in the dark subterranean corridors.

Suddenly, the lights returned. The officers and men, who were first to get into the open, were in time to see a great orange light climbing away vertically, before shooting off at high speed. The soldiers examined the unconscious sentry while the other was still crouched in hiding and crying hysterically.

Both men were found to have 'first-and deep second-degree burns—mostly on areas that had been protected by clothes.' The sentry who had retained consciousness was in deep nervous shock and many hours were to pass before he could talk.

The fort's electric clocks had stopped at 2:03 a.m., which suggested that the whole nightmare experience had lasted no more than about four minutes.

Later that morning, the colonel in command of Fort Itaipu issued orders forbidding the communication of the incident to anyone. Intelligence officers were quickly at work conducting an investigation, and a report was sent to army headquarters. Some days later, officers from the UFS military mission arrived, together with the Brazilian Air Force officers. Meanwhile, the sentries were flown to Rio de Janeiro and admitted to the Army Central Hospital, where a security net was promptly drawn around them. Three weeks later, an officer from the fort, who was interested in UFO reports, sought out Dr Olavo Fontes, who was involved in the investigation of the famous Antonio Vilas Boas case. The officer had been present at the fort during the incident, and gave Fontes full details of the case. Dr Fontes approached the medical colleagues at the hospital, who confirmed that two soldiers were being treated for severe burns, but would tell him nothing more about their case.

Without further corroboration, Dr Fontes could not publish an account. So the case lingered in the files until mid 1959, when, by chance, the doctor met three other officers who in the course of conversation confirmed what had happened. Thanks to the unauthorised disclosures due to which the world has some knowledge, though tantalisingly incomplete, of a UFO's unwelcome visit to Fort Itaipu on that terrifying night.

16. Jimmy Carter's UFO Sighting

It occurred on January 6, 1969, in Leary, Georgia, at about 7:15 p.m., the former U.S. president, Jimmy Carter, who was at the time governor of Georgia, was standing outdoors waiting to address the local Lions Club. A group of about a dozen people were with him. Here is the president's report as quoted in the *National Enquirer*, June 8, 1976:

"I am convinced that UFOs exist because I've seen one. It was a very peculiar aberration, but about 20 people saw it. It was the darndest thing I've ever seen. It was big; it was very bright; it changed colours; and it was about the size of the moon. We watched it for 10 minutes, but none of us could figure out what it was."

In October 1973, Governor Carter filled out a detailed report form for the National Investigations Committee on Aerial Phenomena (NICAP). In it, he estimated the object to have been about 30 degrees above the horizon, as bright as but somewhat smaller than the moon and perhaps, at a distance of 300 to 1000 metres. He said that it moved closer and then further away several times before disappearing.

17. Tasmanian Experience

A wave of 'nocturnal lights' flooded Tasmania from February through October 1974. The earlier sightings were from the north and northwestern part of the island, while the later sightings, from May through October, were mainly from the northeastern portion. Here are some of the more interesting reports.

On February 25, in the Derwent Valley area, Mr. M. noticed a round light in the northeastern sky about 4:20 in the morning. The glow increased in brilliance and soon the witness saw directly above his car a dazzling white light with a flat surface and an ill-defined orange ring near the outer edge. Mr. M. estimated the UFO to be 5 m in width. The UFO 'paced' his car for many kilometres before it disappeared.

On February 27, at 9:45 p.m. near Latrobe, Greg Thornton and his girlfriend, Sally Lamprey, saw an orange dot in the sky move towards their car. It increased in size to about the diameter of a tennis ball and looked like 'a triangle with rounded corners' at first. Later on, it turned on its side and 'appeared as a straight orange line, like a pencil at a 45 degree angle.'

Another witness also saw the same object a few minutes later. Judging from its apparent size and distance, he estimated it to have an actual diameter of 6 metres.

On May 25, three witnesses from Boobyalla Estate (a group of houses and stockyards) saw from their car what they first thought to be the moon but soon realised it was a strange, stationary light "shaped roughly like a large banana, but fatter in the middle. It was a bright orange below, and more of a fire-red in the middle, blending to bright yellow on top. The object was only 6 m above the ground." It began to move towards the witnesses to about 60 metres in front of them. They estimated the UFO to be approximately 30 m long. They were frightened and left the area.

Two nights later (May 27), about a dozen residents of Boobyalla saw the same or a remarkably similar object, and described this as a banana or a half-moon on its side. All the witnesses agreed that it was low to the ground and emitted a strong glow that lit up the cattle pens.

18. First Martyr of Ufology

Captain Thomas Mantell Jr. is described by many as the first martyr of Ufology. In January 1948, Captain Thomas Mantell was part of a flight of four P51 Mustang aircraft belonging to the National Guard and flying between Georgia and Kentucky.

Godman Air Force Base in Kentucky radioed the flight and asked them to investigate a UFO sighting near the base. Of the four pilots, one, Hendricks, continued his heading and landed at Standiford Field while the remaining three pilots, Hammond, Clements and Mantell, climbed to 7500 m in pursuit. Apparently because of lack of oxygen, Hammond and Clements called off the pursuit and continued on their way, safely landing at Standiford Field, some forty minutes behind their colleague.

Mantell continued the pursuit. It is alleged that he radioed the tower, "It appears to be a metallic object, tremendous in size, directly ahead and slightly above. I am trying to reach close for a better look."

A few minutes later Mantell was dead, his plane wrecked and strewn across the ground, some 3 km south-west of Frankly, Kentucky.

The official report on the Mantell crash alleges that he lost consciousness while suffering from anoxia (oxygen deprivation) because of climbing too high, and it was likely he was 'chasing' the planet Venus. Another suggestion has been made that he 'locked on to' a rogue weather balloon. Speculation has always been intense that Mantell was engaged and destroyed by deliberate, intelligent intent.

The case has always been shrouded by mystery, much of it unwarranted. For example, it was alleged that his funeral was held as 'closed coffin' because his body was not there, having not been in the plane when it was recovered. There is no evidence for this and although an open casket before a funeral is traditional in some parts of the United States, that is rarely the case for plane crash victims for obvious reasons. Other stories report that the body was recovered and found to have extraordinary and inexplicable wounds. Again, there is no documentary support for this. Even the statement that Mantell reported the object as "metallic.....tremendous in size", while documented, could have been the result of his oxygen-starved perceptions.

That said, Mantell was an experienced pilot and it seems unlikely he could have been so swept along by the tide of a flying saucer publicity and died chasing Venus because of it.

19. In Terms of Size

An astonishing report, in terms of size, at least, came from Captain Kenju Terauchi of Japan Air Lines who was flying over Alaska in November 1986. During final preparations for landing at Anchorage Airport, Terauchi and his crew on the cargo transportation flight noticed lights accompanying their Boeing 747 'jumbo' jet.

Terauchi had only a short while to examine the silhouette of the object, which appears to have been partly saucer-shaped but more or less spherical and at least twice the size of an aircraft carrier.

The encounter was tracked by radar, and air traffic control instructed the pilot to make certain turns, possibly to avoid the object, which continued to pace the plane for over half an hour before disappearing.

Terauchi speculated in the most humorous way on the possibility that the encounter was extraterrestrial. He stated, "We were carrying beverages from France to Japan. Maybe, they wanted to drink it."

On January 11, 1987, Terauchi had a second encounter with a UFO but he described this as quite different. This time the lights appeared three times below his craft and occasionally behind it.

20. Wing-shaped Craft

A whole series of nocturnal lights, some of them having the general outlines of a wing-shaped "craft," was reported in and around Lubbock, Texas, in 1951, during the months of August and September. Hundreds of people saw the lights and one man photographed them. They were also tracked on radar.

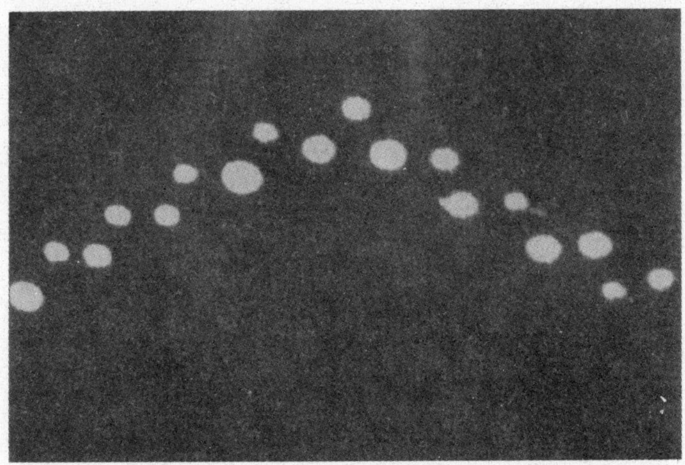

The first sighting was made over Albuquerque, New Mexico, on the evening of August 25, 1951. An employee of the Atomic Energy Commission and his wife reported watching a huge "wing-shaped" UFO, with bluish lights on the rear edge, pass overhead. According to them, the UFO was only

250 to 300 metres up. They could see that the "wing" was sharply swept back and was about 1½ times the size of a B36. Dark bands ran from the front to the back and the "wing light" was softly glowing blue-green.

On the evening of the New Mexico sighting, but somewhat later, several college professors sitting on a porch in Lubbock, Texas, saw a roughly semicircular formation of light sweep rapidly overhead. After several hours, the lights reappeared and were observed to be softly glowing, bluish objects moving in a more open formation than the first time. That same night, a woman in Lubbock also saw what she called a giant "winglike" craft with bluish lights on the back moving silently over her house. This report was only minutes after the sighting in Albuquerque, about which the woman could not possibly have known.

During the next two weeks in Lubbock, the fast moving night-lights were seen on several occasions. Observers agreed that the "flights" always appeared about 45 degrees above the northern horizon, travelled through 90 degrees of the sky often in just over three seconds, and disappeared about 45 degrees above the southern horizon. Among the viewers was a Dr. George, a physics professor who had made extensive studies of the atmosphere and, along with the other professors, could not arrive at a scientific explanation of what they had all seen.

Probably, the same lights were photographed by an amateur photographer named Carl Hart, Jr., on the evening of August 31. One of his photographs, showing a series of bright disk-like objects in a roughly V-shaped formation against the night sky, appeared in a local newspaper.

The air force made thorough investigation of the Lubbock "lights" but could never arrive at a satisfactory explanation. The Hart negatives proved to be genuine, and dozens of witnesses confirmed sightings of soft, bluish lights zipping from one horizon to the other. Sometimes the objects—reportedly from three to several dozens in number –were in precise V-formation, but at other times, they appeared in more random arrangements. Such "natural" causes as reflections from newly installed mercury-vapour street lamps or reflections from the glistening white chests of flying birds (plovers) were suggested to explain the lights. However, these hardly seemed likely to those who observed them.

21. Creatures in the Court

Marius Dewilde's home was situated among the woods and fields less than one- and- half kilometre from the French village of Quarouble near the Belgian border. Despite the fact that the 'National Coal Mines' railroad tracks ran along one side of Dewilde's property, the nights were tranquil. During such quiet times, after his wife and son were usually in bed, the French steelworker would sit in the kitchen and read the newspaper before retiring himself. The night of September 10, 1954, however, was different.

Hearing the family's dog barking and howling, Dewilde suspected a prowler. Taking his flashlight, he went to investigate. Outside, he spotted something near the railroad tracks, but assumed it was a farmer's truck.

As the dog cringed up to him on its stomach, the steelworker was suddenly startled by a sound to his right. Swinging around. he caught a glimpse of an odd sight: two creatures with very broad shoulders, but no arms, and wearing what appeared to be diving suits and helmets. No more than a meter tall, the creatures seemed to shuffle on short legs. They were heading for the dark shape, he thought was merely a truck.

Dewilde ran to the garden gate, intending to cut the creatures off. Suddenly a blinding beam of light from the dark shape on the tracks struck and immobilised him. He wasn't even about to shout as he saw the creatures pass within a metre of him and head toward the tracks.

The light was quickly extinguished, however, and Dewilde continued his chase, but it was too late. The creatures apparently reached their destination. The dark shape rose with a whistling noise as it discharged a cloud of steam beneath. Reaching a height of about 10 metres, the craft then took off towards the east, climbing higher and glowing red as it did so.

Shaken, Dewilde ran to report the incident to the police, who dismissed him as crazy. The commissioner, however, realised that he was neither mad nor joking and initiated a detailed inquiry. Investigators initially suggested that Dewilde might have suffered a hallucination, the result of a head injury.

That may have been discounted had they paid attention to the deeply cut marks in the iron hard wood of the railroad cars. A railroad engineer estimated that such marks could have been created only by an object weighing at least thirty tons. It would have taken intense heat, moreover, to burn the ballast stones between the cars.

22. The Car that Flew

On January 21, 1988, Fay Knowles, her three sons, and two dogs, were driving from Perth east towards Mundrabilla across the Nullarbor Plain. At about 1:30 a.m, their car radio began to malfunction. At about 1:45 a.m, the quartet saw lights in the distance. As the car approached, it became clear that there was only one light.

The light was hovering by the side of the highway. Sean Knowles, who was driving, did not realise until the last moment that it was glowing down on another vehicle. He swerved violently to avoid a crash and then hung a 'U' to see what was happening. The light flew on up the road, with the Knowles' vehicle in hot pursuit. Then the light began to head back towards the car. Sean turned again, but the UFO caught up. Something landed on the car roof with a distinct thump, and the vehicle seemed to rise up. Fay Knowles rolled down a window and put her hand out to feel the object above. She said it felt "warm and spongy". Otherwise, there was chaos in the car. One son said that he felt as if his brains were being pulled out of his head. Sean, the driver, passed out briefly. The dogs were going berserk. Dust was swirling in through the open window, and there was a smell of decomposing bodies.

Then the UFO let go of the car. It crashed to the ground, bursting a tire. Sean brought it under control, stopped, and the family jumped out. They hid by the side of the highway until the UFO flew off. They could now see that the light was about the same size as the car, white, with a yellow centre. A kind of electrical hum came from it. When it had gone, one of the weirder effects of the experience emerged: for about 15 minutes, everyone's voice became very high-pitched, as if they had been breathing helium. In this state, the family changed the wheel and drove on to Mundrabilla.

23. He Arrived without Flying Saucer

In England in 1957, a Birmingham housewife claimed to have been visited by a spaceman in her own home. He did not arrive in a flying saucer, but was only accompanied by a whistling sound. He came in the living room of a 27-year-old, Mrs Cynthia Appleton. He was tall and fair and wore a tight-fitting plastic-like garment. According to Mrs Appleton, he communicated by telepathy, and produced T.V-like pictures to illustrate his flying saucer and a larger master craft. He indicated to her that he came from a place of harmony and peace. At the end of all this, he vanished.

24. Was it an Island or UFO?

On January 10, 1958, Captain Chrysologo Rocha was sitting with his wife in the porch of a house overlooking the sea near Curitiba. He was surprised to see an unfamiliar 'island'. He had his binoculars with him. When he had focused on the island, he was amazed to see that it was growing in size. He cried out to people inside the house, and very soon, eight of them joined the couple on the porch to witness the strange phenomenon.

The object seemed to consist of two parts, one in the sea and the other suspended above it. Then, without warning, both parts sank out of sight; soon afterwards a steamer hovered in sight and passed very near the point where the objects were last seen. Fifteen minutes later, when the ship had gone, the 10 observers said the objects rose once again from the sea. Now they could see that the upper section was attached to the lower piece by a number of shafts or tubes, which were quite bright. Up and down the shafts, small objects 'like beads in a necklace' passed in a disorderly fashion. This second display lasted for a few minutes, and the whole thing started to sink, eventually disappearing beneath the waves.

One of the witnesses, the wife of another army officer, telephoned the Forte dos Andrades barracks at Guaraja, and the air force base was alerted. An aeroplane was scrambled to investigate, but arrived on the scene after the objects had disappeared.

25. Buzzing Around USAF

The Royal Air Force bases at Bentwaters and Lakenheath were both leased to the USAF. Any unknown aircraft coming in from the east over the North Sea was reckoned to be potentially hostile. On the night of August 13-14, 1956, several UFOs flying at fantastic speeds were picked up by about six military radars simultaneously, from 9:30 p.m. onwards. The final intrusion was the most dramaticone.

At 10:55 p.m., the ground radar at Bentwaters picked up an unidentified target coming in from the sea at 3200-6450 km/h speeds well beyond the capacity of any conventional aircraft. The UFO flew directly over the base and disappeared from the screen 48 km to the west. A control tower operator saw it pass over, and the pilot of a USAF C-47 at 1200 metres saw a fuzzy light flash from the plane to the ground. The UFO appeared on a radar at Lakenheath, performing aerobatics. The base alerted the RAF, who scrambled a Venom NF2a fighter from RAF Waterbeach. The Venom soon made contact, but the UFO flipped over and came up behind the fighter, which then tried to shake it off without success. A second Venom fighter joined in, but the UFO dropped away. It was last seen on radar heading north at 970 km/h.

26. Face to Face

Aliens will not reveal their mission on Earth until enough people accept the reality of the UFOs, and man can understand them on a technical and scientific basis. Dr Harley Rutledge made this verdict after a seven-year study of the subject.

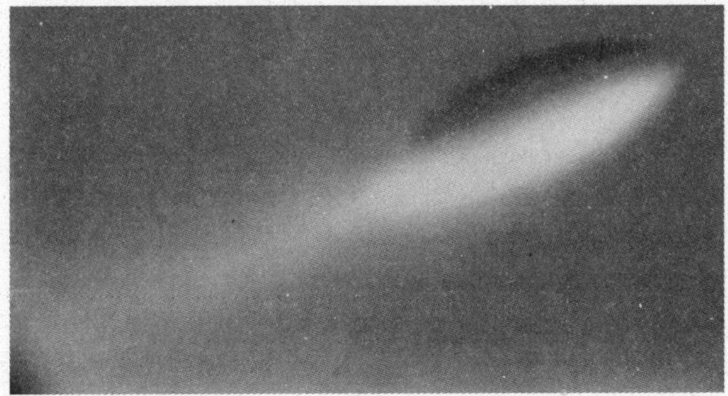

He claims UFOs zip around the Earth constantly, reading our minds and listening to our conversations. But they usually travel so fast that we cannot see them. And they only appear when they want to attract our attention.

Dr Rutledge, chairman of the physics department of the south-western Missouri State University, said he was a sceptic when the study began in 1973. He and nearly 500 helpers spent 2,000 hours studying the sky over three Missouri towns, Cape Giradeau, Piedmont and Farmington, and reported 157 sightings of 178 movements, voices, radio signals and thoughts.

"We sensed that we were dealing with an intelligence," said Dr Rutledge. "I felt as though something was toying with us. On one occasion, we deliberately changed our viewing position and moved 16 km to the west to get directly into the path of UFOs we had been observing. The UFOs changed directions to go a round us, just as they had done before."

He added: "I suspect their game is gradually to create general acceptance by repeated appearance. More UFO flaps will occur from location to location, winning converts."

"When we understand them, and when most of the world's inhabitants accept the reality of UFOs, then we will meet them face to face and know why they are here."

27. Even the Crashed UFO Escaped

On October 31, 1963, an eight-year-old Rute de Souza was playing near her home in Iguape, southwest of Santos (Brazil), when she heard a noise that was growing rapidly louder. Looking around, she saw a silvery object coming down out of the sky, heading towards the nearby Peropava River. After passing over the house, the UFO collided with the top of a palm tree and began to twist, turn and wobble in the air. Then Rute saw it fall into the river close to the far bank.

The child turned to run home, and met her mother who, alarmed by the noise, was running towards the river. Then followed Rute's uncle, Raul de Souza, who had been working about 100 metres from the house. The three of them stood transfixed as they watched the surface of the river. At the spot where the object had sunk, the water was 'boiling up'. This was followed by an eruption of muddy water.

Rute was not the only witness. On the far bank, a number of fishermen had watched the spectacle. One of them, a Japanese gentleman named Tetsuo Iosigawa, gave descriptions of the incident to official investigators and reporters. The object, shaped like a "wash basin", was estimated to have been about 7.5 m in diameter; it had been no more than 6 metres off the ground when it hit the palm tree. The general assumption was that the object was in difficulties after the collision.

The authorities also assumed that a wrecked 'flying saucer' was embedded in the muddy bottom of the river, but driver could find nothing in the water. Finally, engineers searched the area with mine detectors, but they too failed to locate the object.

Speculating about the incident in the *Bulletin* of the Aerial Phenomena Research Organisation (APRO), Jim and Coral Lorenzon wrote that the reported size of the UFO suggested could have carried a crew, and if so, then repairs may have been effected that would have enabled that craft to escape.

28. Aerial Craft over Hawaii

Unidentified flying objects have been in the news, off and on, since the late 1940s. At first, researchers could find no patterns to their appearances. Later, "flying saucers" seemed to show up most often in the northern hemisphere in the spring and summer months. The rest of the years they were more likely to visit the southern half of the world.

In the early sixties, another pattern emerged. The UFOs popped up again and again with satellite launchings and atomic bomb tests. They also seemed to be curious about other aspects of the human technology. For example, Captain Joe Walker spotted and photographed a strange object that followed him as he made a test flight in the rocket plane X-15, soaring thousands of kilometres an hour high in the sky.

While many of these reported UFOs were seen only by one or two people, an incident on March 11, 1963, involved thousands of eyewitnesses. A circular, glowing object followed by a hazy white light soared through the sky for five or six minutes over the island of Hawaii.

Among the people, who saw the strange craft, were two Hawaiian National Guard pilots who reported spying it from their jets as they flew at a 12,000 metres altitude. Lieutenant George Joy noted that the unidentified object had a glowing vapour trail. A Federal Aviation Authority spokesman told newspaper reporters that he and co-workers had also spotted the thing.

Whatever the UFO was, it was clearly not a satellite. And meteors and missiles wouldn't have hovered in the sky for several minutes, while hundreds watched. So the case of the UFO that visited Hawaii remains one more unexplained sighting of unknown aerial craft.

29. Abduction of Betty and Barney Hill

One of the most important and significant UFO sightings and abductions in the UFO lore is the abduction of Betty and Barney Hill.

In September 1961, the Hills were returning from a holiday in Canada to their home in New Hampshire. During the drive late in the evening, near Indian Head, they noticed a bright light in the sky ahead of them. Over a period of time, they noticed that it appeared to pace their car and get much closer. A radar report at the nearby Pease air force base confirmed that there was something moving in the air at that time.

The Hills stopped the car and examined the light through binoculars, believing the object to be structured with various flashing coloured lights.

At a later point during the drive, the object came much closer and Barney left the car, walking across a field to within a close proximity. Through binoculars, he gained the impression that there were people looking back at him and became afraid that he was going to be captured by them. He ran back to his car and rejoined his wife and they drove off in haste.

They arrived home apparently some two hours later than they should have done.

Some two years after the event, they began a programme of *regression hypnosis* under Dr Benjamin Simon, a Boston psychiatrist, to relieve tensions, which they attributed to this encounter.

Under *regression hypnosis,* the couple revealed that they were stopped by the UFO, removed from their car, taken aboard a landed flying saucer and subjected to various forms of medical examination before being released.

Any full analysis of the case must take into account the fact that Betty Hill, in particular, had shown great interest in UFO material in the years intervening between the event and the *regression hypnosis* sessions, and that this material may have affected the recall. Dr Benjamin Simon insisted that any analysis of the event should take account of the fact that under *regression hypnosis,* the subject will tell a story, which is the truth as it appears to the witness but which may not necessarily be an objective truth.

However, any analysis of the case also has to take into account the radar trace at Pease air force base.

During the encounter, Betty Hill reported seeing a 'star map.' Based on this, researcher Marjorie Fish reconstructed a three-dimensional representation of stars in proximity to earth, which would seem to indicate that the aliens came from Zeta Reticuli I and 2.

During regression Betty Hill also revealed that she had been examined by way of a needle through the navel. This is significant because at that time there was no such recognised medical test, whereas in subsequent years, such a test has become prominent.

Betty Hill has been a witness of many encounters. In an interview with John Spencer, she stated that there was a period in her life when she could not go outside her house without being followed by the UFOs in the sky. It has been revealed that in addition to this, Betty has a long history of paranormal experiences, including some particularly impressive precognitive dreams about the violent deaths of friends and acquaintances.

Journalist John G. Fuller in his book, *The Interrupted Journey*, brought her case to the public domain and it remains one of the most impressively documented cases to date.

30. World Famous UFO Film

On December 21, 1978, Captains Verne Powell and John Randle were flying from Blenheim to Christchurch, New Zealand, in an Argosy cargo aircraft, en route to Dunedin, when they became witnesses to several radar and visual sightings of the UFOs. At one point, there were five strong radar targets where none should have been, according to known traffic movements. Throughout the flight, there were several UFO sightings of objects apparently pacing the plane. Captain Randle commented that although he had seen one or two unusual things in his twenty-eight years of pilot experience, they were "nothing as irrational and inexplicable as these latest ones".

Ten days later, on December 31, 1978, Channel O in Melbourne decided to retrace the Argosy's flight in a plane of its own which it chartered for the purpose. There was a film crew on board whose purpose was to film background material for a documentary on the earlier sighting. They were going to get more than they bargained for!

As the film crew were in the loading bay filming background material, the crew suddenly spotted lights in the direction of Kaikoura and radioed Wellington control who told them that there were 'targets' in that position, though they kept appearing and disappearing.

Wellington radar, shortly after midnight, reported another target, which the Argosy was able visually to confirm with the comments: "It's got a flashing light." Twelve seconds of film were taken of this object which has since become world famous.

Throughout the remainder of the flight, there were many other sightings. On the return leg an hour later, now past two o'clock in the morning, another bright UFO was seen and filmed from the aircraft.

Despite the film footage, there has never been a final conclusion drawn on what exactly was seen.

31. Aliens Attack a Farm

On the night of April 22, 1955, there were eight adults and three children at the Sutton farm. Billy Ray Taylor and his wife June were visiting Elmer, the elder of the two Sutton boys. At about 7:00 p.m., Billy Ray went out into the yard to fetch a drink from the well. He saw a gigantic object. It was "real bright, and had all the colours of the rainbow." It landed in a dried-out gulch nearby. But when he told the Suttons what he had seen, no one bothered to go outside and look.

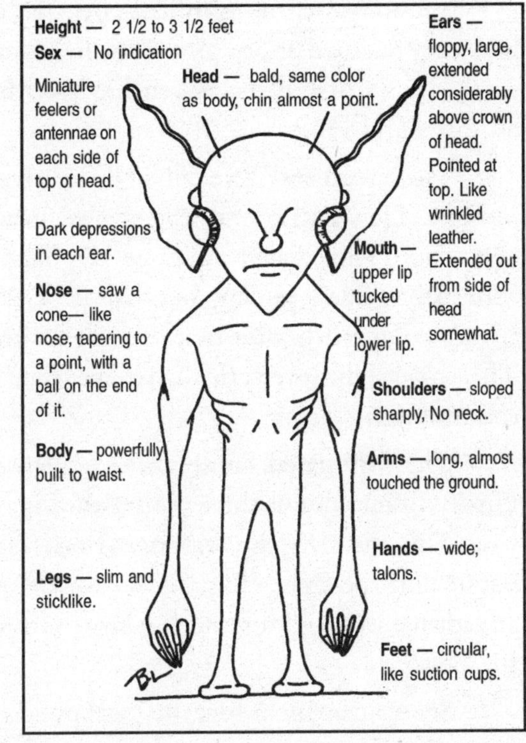

An hour later, the dog began barking in the yard. Elmer and Billy Ray, suspecting intruders, picked up their guns and went to the kitchen door. Slowly approaching the house was a small 'shining' man with his hands held over his head. The men opened fire. The tiny figure somersaulted backwards from the impact of the shots, which hit it with a sound "as if you had shot into a pail". Then it fled.

Several more creatures approached the house from different angles, and were shot at. One was heard on the kitchen roof; Elmer and Billy Ray both fired at it, and it fell, then 'floated' another 12 metres to settle on a fence. The two fired again, simultaneously. The thing fell and then scuttled off into the weeds behind the fence on all fours.

Shooting had no terminal effect on any of the intruders, and they seemed more afraid of the lights from the Suttons' torches than of bullets. When hit by either, they dropped on all fours and ran.

The creatures were all a little over a metre tall when upright. They had round, egg-shaped heads, very large, yellow eyes spaced wide apart, and huge, elephant-like ears. Their long, thin arms ended in claw-like hands. They had slim, straight, silvery-coloured bodies that seemed to be lit from the inside. This inner light intensified whenever they were shot at, or even shouted at.

The frightened family locked themselves into the house. Finally, after about three hours during which the intruders peered in through the windows from time to time, all eight adults and the three children ran for the two cars on the farm and drove to Hopkinsville, 11 km south on route 41, to alert the police.

Six officers including the local police chief returned to the farm with the family and searched the place, but found no sign of the visitors. They left at about 2:00 a.m, and the family went to bed. Then the creatures returned, surrounded the house and peered through the windows. They withdrew at about 5:15 a.m.

32. Delayed Spanish Airline Flight

The Spanish charter airline flight had been delayed four hours before finally taking off from Salzburg, Austria, enroute to Tenerife in the Canary Islands. The passengers' discontent was aggravated further when the plane made an unscheduled landing in Valencia, Spain. It may have been the least of their concerns had they known what precipitated the detour on that Sunday evening in November 1979.

It began after the plane had passed over Ibiza. Shortly before eleven o'clock, Flight Captain Commandant Lerdo de Tejada saw two bright red lights to the left of the aircraft. The object rapidly bore down on the plane from the left and a little behind. "It was moving upwards and downwards at will, all around us and performing movements that would be impossible for any conventional machine," Tejada said. He added that it seemed to be like a jumbo-jet.

The unidentified object followed the aircraft for about eight minutes. About 9.5 km from Valencia, the speed and closeness of the object forced the plane to make a sharp turn to avoid a possible collision. It disappeared after another 50 kilometres.

The airport's director, traffic controller and other personnel confirmed seeing something with red lights. News reporter, Juan Benitez, also learnt later that the Spanish air force had picked up the UFO on a military radar in the same area as the airliner. Minutes after Tejada had landed at Valencia, two air force planes were dispatched and sighted the object. One pilot reported close physical encounters with what he described as the UFO.

33. White Balls of Calcium Carbonate

Three- and- half kilometre outside the small town of Trancas in northwestern Argentina, the Moreno family's Santa Teresa Ranch has its own electric power plant. When it broke down on the evening of October 21, 1963, the household retired early, while twenty-one-year-old Yolie de Valle Moreno stayed awake to feed her infant son.

The house was still and quiet, when the maid, Dora, suddenly knocked on Yolie's door, crying that there were strange lights outside. The whole farmyard seemed to be illuminated. To the east, near the railroad tracks, there were two bright, disk-shaped objects connected by a shining tube. It looked, Yolie said, "like a small train, intensely illuminated." They could also make out a number of shadows moving within the tube. They suspected, at first, that there might have been a derailment.

As they walked around to the front of the house, they saw two pale greenish lights near the gate of the farm. As Yolie directed the flashlight towards it, she realised it was a disk-shaped, domed object, about 10 metres wide. It hung in midair while emitting a slight hum. Through its six windows, the women could see a band of multicoloured lights which began rotating as a white mist enveloping the object. Without warning, flames shot out, knocking the women to the ground.

Next, a tube of light, about 3 metres wide, emerged from the top of the object and probed the features of the house. Three more objects appeared on the railboard tracks and directed 3 metres wide beams of light towards the henhouse, the tractor shed and a neighbour's place. Yolie ran inside where the temperature had risen from 60°F to a stifling 104°F, and the air smelled of sulphur.

After about forty minutes, the object at the farm's gate retracted its light and joined the others on the tracks. Finally, all six objects rose and flew off toward Sierra de Medina, a mountain range to the east.

The cloud, that had enveloped the object nearest to the house, didn't dissipate until four hours later. A journalist, who visited the family, the next day, said the heat and the smell of sulphur still lingered. What's more, a pile of small white balls, forming a perfect one-metre cone, lay beneath the spot where the object had hovered outside the gate.

Similar balls were found on the tracks. Later analysis at the University of Tucuman's Institute of Chemical Engineering determined they were composed mostly of calcium carbonate, with a small percentage of potassium carbonate.

In a later inquiry, half a dozen other members of the community told the local police that they had seen the illuminated objects on the railroad tracks as well. One man said he saw six disk-shaped objects flying across the sky at 10:15 p.m, about the time the Moreno's ordeal ended.

34. Blip of the Largest Aircraft

On the evening of February 19, 1956, in the control room at Orly Airport, Paris, the radar screen suddenly showed a blip with an echo twice as large as that of the largest known aircraft. The radar image behaved in a very erratic manner, slowing down, hovering, and then accelerating dramatically, quite unlike anything the operator had ever seen before.

At that point, a more familiar blip showed up on the screen. It was soon identified as an Air France Douglas Dakota airliner on its regular Paris-London run. The control tower radioed the craft that a UFO was in its path. The radio officer, who received the message, looked through a porthole and was

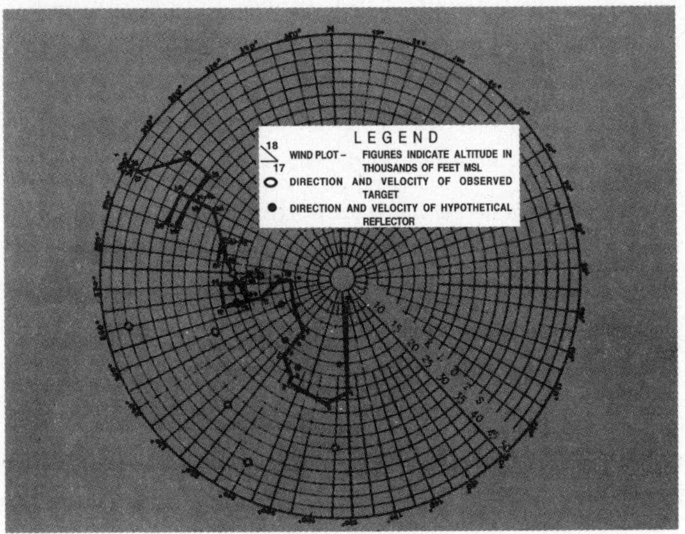

amazed to see an enormous indistinct outline with a red glow. He and the captain watched the UFO for a full half-minute before it disappeared. In his report, the captain stated that the object they saw carried none of the required navigation lights. At Orly, radarmen followed the UFO's strange flight for four hours on their screen. Then it disappeared. An odd twist to this story is that neither El Burgess Airport nor the Paris Observatory picked up this UFO on their radar screens.

35. Planet Earth is Worth Helping

Psychic Greta Woodrew, of Connecticut, claimed she was contacted by aliens, and told that they are waiting to help the Earth cope with future catastrophes.

She said she met beings from a planet called Ogatta, many light years away, during experiments at the Ossining, New York, laboratories of para-psychologist, Dr Andrija Puharich.

The first contact came in December 1976. Mrs Woodrew was put into a deep hypnotic trance. She claimed she found herself in a long shadowy tunnel being guarded by a man-like creature called Hshames and two bird-like 'entities'. Hshames stood just over 1.5 m tall, and his skin was covered with minute feathers. He had large, gold-flecked, luminous, lashless eyes, and his upper lip resembled a beak. They conversed by telepathy, and the figure told her about Ogatta.

During the second experiment, Mrs Woodrew claimed that her soul left her body, and she was transported to Ogatta itself. Everything shone, and the surface was covered with dots like glistening halves of marbles. They held a precious water-like substance.

At the next session, according to Mrs Woodrew, an entity called Ogatta spoke to her. He said, "these beings had set up a waystation on the minor planet, Vesta in our solar system, which will be used to help Earth. An armada of spaceships, called Gattae, would come down to Earth after drastic changes occurred. Their preparations were well under way."

Mrs Woodrew claimed she was then shown scenes of devastation, which could happen to the Earth in the next few decades. Floods, hurricanes, super-magnetic storms, droughts, earthquakes, volcanic eruptions, tidal waves, etc. will cover entire cities, and people will die of thirst and hunger.

"I was told by the extra-terrestrials that they were survivors of what could come," Mrs Woodrew said. "Then they said, 'Despite what man can do to man and the nature's plan, there are civilizations in the cosmos who believe that the planet Earth is worth helping.'"

36. Now I Believe in UFOs

At about 8:30 on the quiet evening of July 12, 1977, Adrian de Olmos Ordonez, forty-two, was resting on the balcony of his home in Quebradillas, Puerto Rico, when he saw something crawl under a barbed-wire fence on a farm not far away. In the dusk, De Olmos could see it was a small figure, apparently a child.

A closer look, however, revealed that this was no normal child at all. The creature wore a bulbous green garment and a metallic helmet, at the top of which was an antenna "with a bright light or flame at its tip."

De Olmos called his daughter Irasema to bring him a pencil and paper so that he could sketch the figure as he watched it. As he would tell Puerto Rican ufologist Sebastian Robiou Lamarche, "I told her to turn on the light in the living room, but she made a mistake and she turned on the outside balcony light instead," De Olmos said. The creature was frightened and fled.

"The minute the balcony light went on, I saw the creature run back instantly towards the barbed-wire fence. It passed under the wire and then stopped," he explained. "It placed its hands on the front part of its belt and then a thing that it had on its back, resembling a knapsack, lit up and emitted a sound like the noise of an electric drill. And then it rose up into the air and made off toward the trees." At that point, the witness's daughter, wife and two sons came out of the house to see the lights from the flying device on the creature's back, as it sailed through the air.

For the next ten minutes, they watched the lights moving from tree to tree, sometimes descending briefly to the ground level. Meanwhile, a group of neighbours joined them and they, too, saw the strange spectacle. Eventually, a second group of lights, presumably from a second humanoid, joined the first, perhaps, De Olmos thought, to help its companion because "the apparatus on the creature's back was not working quite right."

Soon the lights were out, leaving only a badly frightened collection of people who wasted no time in notifying the police. The police conducted an extensive investigation, as did the well-known Puerto Rican ufologist Robiou Lamarche. Reporting on his investigation in Britain's *Flying Saucer Review,* Lamarche wrote, "In the course of our inquiries we ascertained that Sr. Adrian is a serious, well-respected and hard-working person, held in high regard by all the neighbours. He is a businessman, engaged in the distribution of cattle feed throughout the northwestern area of the island. He had never before taken the slightest interest in the UFO phenomenon or in any related subjects. But, he told us, "Now I believe in these things."

37. At Farmington, New Mexico

On March 18, 1950, the entire population of some 5,000 inhabitants, including the mayor, newspapermen and highway patrolmen at Farmington, New Mexico, watched "hundreds of strange objects" performing aerial acrobatics in the sky for more than an hour in the late morning. Some of the objects, described as spaceships, flying at speeds calculated at more than 1,600 km/h, participated in the flying exercise. The UFOs disappeared before noon but were back again in the afternoon. Newspapers reported "incredible manoeuvrability and acute control in split-second timing by their ability to avoid collisions."

38. Stubborn Bureaucracy

One of the most celebrated sightings of the UFO was reported by Jimmy Carter in 1969, some years before his ascendency to the presidency of the United States. President Carter reported the object as being approximately the size of the moon. It was very bright and changed colours.

The sighting led Carter to claim that he would "make every piece of information this country has about UFO sightings available to the public and the scientists," if he became the president. He apparently tried to fulfil his pledge but found that the stubborn bureaucracy of the various government agencies can be obstructive even to a president. Whether Carter saw this pledge as a vote-catcher or not is a speculation, but we should remember that many witnesses to the UFOs have found their 'world-view' changed by even distant sightings.

39. An Extraordinary Object

Pauld Trent photographed a strange disk-shaped object on May 11, 1950, in Oregon. The two photographs are of great importance in Ufology because of their clarity and the amount of research undertaken to establish their credibility. The present consensus is that an extraordinary object of the kind described below did indeed fly within the view of Mr. and Mrs. Paul Trent.

What the Trents observed on their farm in the township of McMinnville, Oregon, was "a strange thing like a very large lid of a dustbin, with a sort of spur on the top of the curved rim over it." Mr. Trent said the flying object was "shining like burnished silver, was noiseless, and gave off no smoke or vapour. After a few minutes, it went off to the northwest and vanished over the skyline." He saw it in the evening and estimated it to have been about 9 metres in diametre.

When it first came into view, it was flying slowly but did not seem to be rotating.

40. The World's Reaction

The chief of the local gendarmerie questioned Masse soon after his experience was made public. Crowds of sightseers visited the field, and Valensole was flooded with representatives of the press, radio and television. On July 4, overwhelmed with interviews and questions, Masse collapsed and seized with an insuperable desire to sleep. Aime Michel reported that he would have slept 24 hours a day had his wife not awakened him to make him eat.

A local magistrate, who handed his report to *Flying Saucer Review* in October 1965, conducted the initial private investigations. He said that Masse had prevented his daughter approaching too close to the hole, for he feared she might suffer some harmful effect from it. Indeed, he was worried about possible genetic effects it might have on himself. In the end, he filled the hole, which was shaped like an inverted funnel.

Aime Michel interviewed the witness twice at Valensole in 1965, and found him anxious and distressed, still worried about possible effects on his health. During his second visit, Michel showed Masse a photograph of a model based on Lonnie Zamora's description of the UFO, he had seen at Socorro, New Mexico, in 1964. Masse was staggered that someone should have photographed his machine; but when told that a policeman had seen it in the USA, he sighed with relief: "You see then that I wasn't dreaming, and that I'm not mad."

Two years later, the UFO investigators visited Maurice Masse again and he took them to see the landing site. It was 3 metres in diametre and distinguishable because lavender plants around the perimeter were withered, and only weeds grew in the inner area despite the fact that it had been ploughed and replanted.

Although Masse had recovered from his experience, he was anxious to avoid any more publicity. In an endeavour to hide the location of the landing site, he trimmed the mass of weeds to the shape of levender plants. Eventually, he tore up the vineyard, ploughed the lavender field and sowed it all with wheat.

41. The Man who Shot a Spacecraft Passenger

One of the strangest close encounters ever took place on a cold November night in 1961. The witnesses were four North Dakota men driving home from a hunting trip as freezing rain beat down on the windshield of their car. The heating system had nearly given out and the rain turned to ice on the windows. Three of the travellers were asleep and only the driver, who was awake, saw a blazing object descending out of the sky.

It came down three-quarters km away, on the right side of the highway. The driver, alarmed, nudged the sleeping man on the passenger side and he revived quickly enough to see the object, too. So did one of the sleepers in the backseat. All were certain they were witnessing a plane crash.

They sped to the scene, where they found a silo-shaped object sticking at about an eighty-five-degree angle from the ground and 150 metres away. Four figures stood around it, trying to make all this out on a dark night and at some distance made for serious eyestrain. Thus, the men in the car plugged a hand spotlight into the cigarette lighter and shined it on the craft and its occupants. At this point, as one of the hunters later told an investigator for the National Investigations Committee on Aerial Phenomena, "there was an explosion and everything went out."

The men were horrified. They thought the plane had blown up and began driving into the field. But as they approached the site, the craft was nowhere to be found.

Now they awoke the fourth man, a medic at a local air force base, and told him that once they found the "accident" site they would need his help. The medic urged them to go back to where they had been when they first saw the object. That way, he said, they could retrace their steps and make another guess as to where the plane had gone down.

Soon after, they returned to the highway. They saw the object and its occupants again. The medic turned on the spotlight and ran it up and down the silvery, silo-shaped vehicle. Then his light hit one of the figures, a human-shaped form about 1.6 m tall and dressed in white coveralls. Strangely, he was waving his arm in a get-out-of-here gesture. If there had been a plane crash, the witness wondered, why was this man signalling them to leave?

The hunters drove a short distance, arguing all the while about what they should do next. Someone thought the objects was an air force test device that they weren't supposed to see. One argued that the figure was a farmer and the "plane" was a silo. Eventually, they resumed their journey home. They drove 3 more kilometres when the object returned and gently landed less than 150 metres away. Suddenly, two figures were visible in front of the car.

One of the hunters got down to a prone position with a rifle and squeezed off a shot. The closer figure was hit in the shoulder. He spun around and fell to his knees. As his companion helped him up, he hollered, "Now what the hell did you do that for?"

The four men later tried to reconstruct what happened next, and realised their memories were hazy at best. Two of them would deny that a rifle had been taken out of the car at all. The man who remembered shooting the figure said his behaviour seemed irrational and bizarre. The only clear memory they had was that of arriving home just as it was becoming daylight, their worried wives sitting in wait.

The next day, the medic-man, who had fired the shot, was surprised to find some strange men waiting for him at work. Addressing him by name, they said they had "received a report" about his experience the night before. They asked if he had got out of the car during the first part of the experience, and they also wanted to know what he had been wearing. When he answered a hunting gear and boots, they asked him to take them to his home to examine the clothes.

After examining the gear, they got up to leave. The one who had done most of the talking thanked him for his cooperation, then warned, "You'd better not say anything about this to anyone from now on." The men got into their car and drove off, leaving the medic stranded. He had to call a cab to get back to the base.

"They never asked anything about the shooting and all their questions were concerned entirely with the first part of the sighting," the medic remembered. "I think they probably knew more than they said, but I don't know."

He never saw them again. To this day, he has no idea who they were and exactly what they wanted from him.

42. Curious Encounter with a UFO

On the day after George Adamski died, April 24, 1965, a retired prison officer named E.A. Bryant had a curious encounter with a UFO. He was walking near Dartmoor about 5.30 p.m. when a flying saucer appeared out of thin air. It swung back and forth like a clock pendulum, hovered above the ground before coming to rest. An opening appeared in the side and three figures dressed in divingsuits came out. One beckoned to Bryant and as he approached, they removed their headgear. The two had fair hair and blue eyes, and their foreheads seemed too high to be merely human. The third was dark and had an ordinary human face.

The dark one talked to Bryant in a foreign accented English, and apparently said that his name was 'Yamski, and that he wished someone called 'Des' or 'Les' was there to see him because he would understand everything. He explained that he and the others were from the planet, Venus. After the UFO took off, some metallic fragments were found on the ground near the place where it had been.

The report of the experience led the UFO enthusiasts to speculate that the dark-haired visitor had been George Adamski – or his ghost – and that the 'Des' or 'Les' he referred to was his collaborator, Desmond Leslie.

43. 1897 Airship Flap

Human conquest of the skies supposedly began on a December's day in 1903 when Orville and Wilbur Wright, who were brothers and bicycle mechanics, first flew their flimsy biplane a few centimetres above the sand dunes at Kitty Hawk. But in November 1896, seven years before the brief but monumental flight, something apparently man-made was seen in the skies over San Francisco. By April of the following year, when reports peaked, the great airship of 1897 had been sighted on both coasts and throughout the heartland of the nation, from Chicago to Texas.

Hardly a community was spared. Yet the ubiquitous 1897 airship has never been satisfactorily explained. Historians of "official" aviation dismiss it as beneath contempt. But the pages of the newspapers of the day headlined the mystery airship in terms surprisingly reminiscent of latter-day UFOs. Even folklorists and sociologists are hard pressed to explain the prevalence of the reports.

Typically, the sightings fell into two categories: Some people described only nocturnal lights and beams of bright illumination. Others reported a magnificent flying machine crewed by an odd assortment of individuals. The ship was often reported stranded in the countryside, usually in need of simple repairs, before continuing on its way.

There was so much speculation about the airship's origins that famous inventors like Thomas Alva Edison regularly called press conferences to deny the contrivance was theirs.

However, other less honourable inventors did claim the airship as their own, though they were never able to produce a working model on demand. By the fall of 1897, however, airship reports dropped off dramatically, and by the turn of the century, they had virtually disappeared.

Nevertheless, students of anomalous phenomena continue to debate the significance of the great airship to this day. Charles Fort, America's greatest cataloguer of the odd and unusual, suggested that the flying machine was simply an idea whose time had come.

Others believe that the great airship of 1897 somehow spurred the subsequent advances in aviation technology. The Wright brothers may not have been innocent innovators, these pundits argue, but rather the unwitting tools of an unconscious evolutionary urge. This outward impulse, some even suggest, is mirrored in the prevalence of today's UFO reports.

44. Identical Daytime Sightings

During October 1952, two remarkable and almost identical daylight sightings took place at the towns of Oloron-Ste.-Marie and Gaillac in southwestern France. The sightings occurred within 10 days of each other, and hundreds of people witnessed both events.

On October 17, at about 12:50 p.m., Monsieur Yves Prigent, the general superintendent of the Oloron High School, was preparing to sit down to lunch with his wife and children when one child, lingering at the window, suddenly yelled out: "Oh papa, come look, it's fantastic!" The rest of the family rushed to the window and this is Monsieur Prigent's account of what they saw:

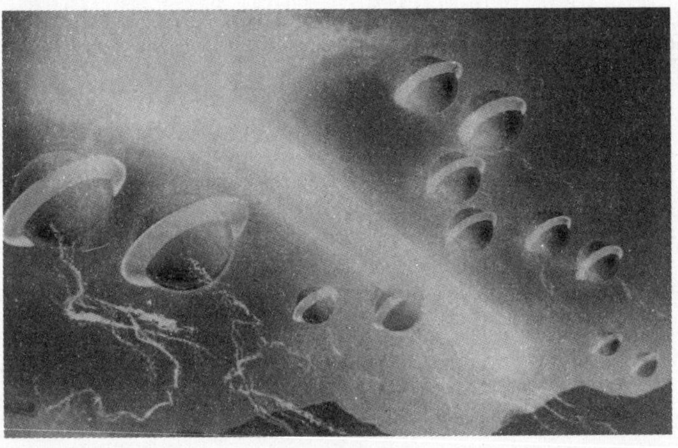

"In the north, a cottony cloud of strange shape was floating against the blue sky. Above it, a long narrow cylinder, apparently inclined at a 45° angle, was slowly moving in a straight line towards the southwest. I estimated its altitude as 2 or 3

kilometres. The object was whitish, non-luminous and very distinctly defined. A sort of plume of white smoke was escaping from its upper end. At some distance in front of the cylinder, about thirty other objects were following the same trajectory. To the naked eye, they appeared as featureless balls resembling puffs of smoke. But with the help of opera glasses, it was possible to make out a central red sphere, surrounded by a sort of yellowish ring inclined at an angle. The angle was such as to conceal almost entirely the lower part of the central sphere, while revealing its upper surface. These "saucers" moved in pairs, following a broken path characterised in general by rapid and short zigzags. When two saucers drew away from one another, a whitish streak, like an electric arc, was produced between them.

All these strange objects left an abundant trail behind them, which slowly fell to the ground as it dispersed. For several hours, clumps of it hung in the trees, on the telephone wires, and on the roofs of the houses.

These gossamer like fiber, sometimes found in conjunction with the UFO sightings, are referred to as angel hair. They resemble wool or nylon thread but tend to disintegrate rapidly.

On October 27 at 5 p.m., a similar spectacle was seen in the sky at Gaillac, a town 240 km distant from Oloran-Ste-Marie. About a hundred witnesses gave the same description of the 20-minutes-long event:

A long plumed cylinder, inclined at 45°, progressed slowly to the southeast in the midst of a score of "saucers" which shone in the sun and flew two by two in a rapid zigzag fashion. The only difference in the Gaillac sighting was that here some pairs of saucers occasionally descended quite low, to an altitude estimated by the observers as 300-400 metres.

Again the witnesses saw angel hair fall and again this substance disappeared soon after it was collected.

45. UFOs Over the White House

One criticism levelled at the UFOs asks why, if they exist, haven't they landed on the White House lawn and made themselves known? Aside from the fact that their occupants might not have found a presidential administration to their liking, the UFOs have appeared in close proximity to the Pennsylvania Avenue on more than one occasion.

Unidentified flying objects, for example, peppered radar screens in the nation's Capital late on the night of July 26, 1952. At one point as many as twelve separate targets were picked up: four, spaced a kilometre-and-a-half apart, proceeded in an orderly pace at a speed of 160 km/h, while eight other moved randomly about at higher speeds.

At least two military personnel and a commercial pilot bound for Washington National Airport reported visual contact with white and orange-white lights in the night sky.

On January 11, 1965, both military and civilian personnel reported the UFOs over the White House. Immediately prior to that, on December 29, 1964, three unknown targets had been tracked on radar at speeds established at almost 8,000 km/h. The air force later discounted the incidents as due to mechanical malfunction.

Eight days before, one Horace Burns said his car stalled on the U.S highway—150 in the presence of a large, cone-shaped UFO. Measuring 38 m wide and 22 m high, the UFO sat in an adjoining field for more than a minute-and-a half before leaving "at a square angle." Professor Ernest Gehman and two DuPont engineers, subsequently, examined the site for radiation and found the levels much above normal.

In fact, five other sightings of the UFOs over or near Washington were reported between October 1964 and January 1965 alone. On January 25, the policemen in Marion, Virginia, saw a glowing and hovering object that departed in a shower of sparks. Twenty minutes later, nine people in Fredericksburg, 480 km away, also reported a bright light, leaving a trail of sparks.

46. UFO Photograph

Dave and Hannah McRobertses were driving on British Columbia's Vancouver Island when they decided, at about noon, to pull over the Eve River Rest Area. Off in the distance, the couple could see a rugged mountaintop set off against the sky by a white cloud, just the scenic view that Hannah thought would make a pretty snapshot.

Hannah focused her camera and took a single photo. A few weeks later, in October 1981, the film was developed. The mountain scene came out clear and scenic. But there was something odd about the photo, something the McRobertses didn't remember seeing when the picture was taken—a silvery disk flying through the sky.

The McRobertses quickly contacted the Canadian National Defences office at Comox about the UFO they had inadvertently captured on film. The army wasn't interested. However, the photo fascinated friends and neighbours. McRobertses soon made more copies of the picture and distributed them to anyone who wanted one.

A copy of the snapshot came to the attention of psychologist Richard Haines in Pasadena, California. Haines, president of the North American UFO Federation, decided to find out more about the photo. He visited the McRobertses at their Campbell River home, examined and tested their camera, and then investigated the area where the photograph had been taken.

In July 1984, Haines told an audience at the Rocky Mountain UFO Conference at the University of Wyoming that, based on his investigation and a computer analysis of the photo, he had come to believe that the saucer-shaped object was real.

He noted that a blowup of the UFO revealed a clear dome on top of the disk. But there's still no explanation of exactly what Hannah McRoberts accidentally caught on the film. "It remains unidentified," Haines concludes.

47. Case Handled with Secrecy

Brazil seems to have had more than its share of the UFO incidents in which witnesses have suffered injury or even death. Only a few years after Inacio de Souza's disastrous experience, another Brazilian came to harm in a brief and terrifying encounter with a mysterious object. The victim on this occasion was Almiro Martins de Freitas, a security watchman who was on duty at the time.

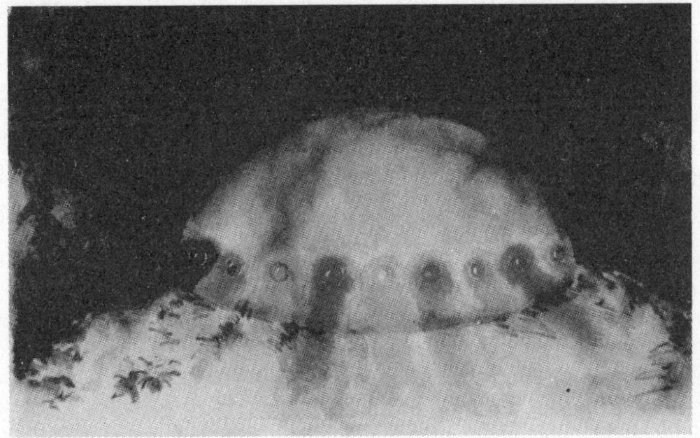

The incident occurred at 9:30 p.m. on August 30, 1970. De Freitas, a married man with three children, was working for the Special Internal Security Patrol services on the Funil Dam at Itatianina, in the state of Rio de Janerio. On this evening, he was out on patrol, inspecting the area for which he was responsible. Heavy rain had just fallen and the ground was wet. He had almost come to the end of his beat when he saw a humpshaped mass on a mound, displaying a row of multicoloured lights. Orange, red and blue were among the colours of the light that the object was emitting.

De Freitas felt uneasy, but he overcame his first instinctive urge to retreat as fast as possible. He began to move cautiously towards the object. Even when he had come to a distance of about 15 m from the object, its shape was still unclear to him in the darkness.

At this point an intense noise assailed his ears. It was like the sound of a jet engine, and it deafened him. Startled, he drew his revolver and started firing towards the lights. After his second shot there was a dazzling flash from the object, seemingly aimed at the security guard. De Freitas was blinded. He fired a third shot wildly, and then a wave of heat engulfed him. He found that he was immobilised.

Shortly afterwards another watchman and a passing motorist arrived at the spot. They found De Freitas was standing stiffly by a mound of the earth, brandishing his revolver and shouting warnings to them: "Don't look! Beware of the flash! It's blinded me!' The two newcomers contrived to carry the stricken man to the car. After a while, he began to recover his ability to move, but he did not recover his sight.

A significant fact supporting De Freitas's account was noticed at the scene of the incident. At the place where he had seen the multicoloured lights, there was a circular area of the ground, despite the downpour that had soaked the ground elsewhere.

From Itatiania, the security guard was taken to a hospital in the city of Guanabara, where psychiatrists and ophthalmologists subjected him to psychological and physical examination. These tests showed that, physiologically, the patient was perfectly normal. His blindness, the investigators decided, had been brought about by shock. De Freitas became noticeably disturbed whenever he talked about the experience.

On September 3, the incident found its way into a number of Brazilian newspapers. At the time of these reports, although a full three-day had elapsed, De Freitas had still not recovered his vision.

From this point, the investigations were taken over by the government's security authorities, and the department assigned to study UFOs played a major role in it. The civilian UFO researchers, who attempted to find out more about the case, found that the official investigation was being handled with an air of secrecy. Evidently, the Brazilian government took seriously this latest incident in the string of violent events involving the UFOs intruding into its national territory.

48. A Banana Grower Goes Banana!

George Pedley, a banana grower of Tully, north Queensland, Australia, was driving his tractor through Albert Pennisis's neighbouring cane farm at 9 a.m. on January 19, 1966, when he saw a " spaceship" rise out of Horseshoe Lagoon, a swamp

about 25 m in front of him. He described the ship as bluish-grey in colour, about 8 m wide and 3 m high. Pedley also reported:

"It spun at a terrific rate as it rose vertically to about 18 m, then made shallow a dive and rose sharply. Travelling at a fantastic speed, it headed off in a southwesterly direction. It was out of sight in seconds."

When Pedley investigated the spot where the UFO was seen, he found a depressed circular area about 9 m in diameter. Within the circle, the reeds were without exception bent below the water level, dead and swirled around in a clockwise manner, as if they had been subjected to some terrific rotary force.

Pedley later said that he had noticed a sulphurous odour in the area around the "nest" after the UFO departed.

Investigation of the circular area revealed a 25- cm layer of reeds within it, torn out by the roots and floating on 2 m of water. Three large holes were discovered under the "nest." These were thought to be "landing indentations." Two other "nests" were later discovered only 25 m from the first one.

The official verdict was that the "nests" were "the results of severe turbulence, which normally accompanies line squalls and thunderstorms prevalent in north Queensland at that time of the year." The weather, however, was fine that day.

49. Hudson Valley Boomerang

The largest mass-sighting incident in the UFO history began in 1982 on New Year's Eve, inundating the Hudson valley in New York, particularly Westchester and Putnam counties. By the summer of 1987, more than five thousand people had seen (and in many cases photographed and videotaped) a huge, triangular-shaped UFO outlined in lights that became known as the "Hudson Valley Boomerang."

Most of the sightings fell within the years 1983 and 1984. Motorists on the Taconic Parkway would frequently pull their cars to the side of the road staring up at a gigantic, slow-moving, silent object that many described in terms of football fields rather than metres. One stunned witness said it was as large as an aircraft carrier. Another compared it to a "flying city."

In spite of the number of authentic photographs and reliable witnesses that included pilots, engineers, and corporate executives, sceptics rashly declared the case "solved." The culprits were supposedly a group of private pilots who, in direct violation of FAA regulations, gathered together in the evenings to scare the living daylights out of local residents. The "Martians," as they called themselves, reportedly flew their Cessnas in tight, night formations to give the illusion of a large, lighted object, manoeuvring overhead.

The only problem with the sceptical "solution" was that several witnesses filmed both the "Martians" and the UFO in flight, and the difference was easily distinguishable. Other witnesses said Cessnas could plainly be heard, whereas the UFO was eerily quiet. Moreover, the huge, illuminated boomerang hovered over the local nuclear power plant, an acrobatic achievement that civilian Cessnas, no matter how accomplished their pilots have yet to manage.

Finally, if the sceptics feel they've really solved the case of the Hudson Valley UFO, they are morally obligated to turn the offenders over to the authorities for proper punishment.

Otherwise, we're forced to conclude that giant, unidentified flying objects lie outside the present jurisdiction of the Federal Aviation Administration.

50. Motor Boat Turned into UFO

On Sunday, June 27, 1970, Senhor Aristeu Machado and his five daughters were playing a game on the *verandah* of their home, 318 Avenida Niemeyer, Rio de Janeiro, from which they could look out over the road below to the South Atlantic Ocean beyond. With them was their friend and neighbour, Senhor Joao Aguiar, an official of the Brazilian Federal Police.

Dona Maria Nazare, who was preparing lunch in the kitchen, called out to check the time: it was 11.38 a.m. About two minutes after that, Senhor Aguiar happened to look out over the sea, and quickly drew the attention of the others to 'a motor boat striking the water'. As this object descended, it threw up spray on all sides.

The game and lunch were quickly forgotten for, as the

family and their guest watched the 'motor boat' they could see two 'bather' aboard the craft, who seemed to be signalling with their arms. In a statement to Dr Walter Buhler, who investigated the case, Aguiar said there were definitely two persons on board and that they were wearing 'shining clothing, and something on their heads. The craft was of greyish metallic colour; it seemed to be between 4.5 and 6 m in length and had a transparent cupola. One strange feature was noted: that at no time did the object make the "bobbing" movement associated with a boat on a swell.

Sr. Aguiar ran down to the nearby Mar Hotel and telephoned the Harbour police; they promised to send help to the occupants of the 'motor boat', who were presumably involved in a mishap offshore. Aguiar then returned to the house and rejoined the Machados on their *verandah.* He had been away from the house for about 30 minutes.

Shortly after Aguiar returned, the object, which was now seen to be disk-shaped, took off. It had been on the surface for 40 to 45 minutes. It skimmed the water for some 300 metres, throwing off a wave from the bows as it went, then lifted from the water and made off quickly towards the south-east. It was then that the witnesses realised that it was not a motor boat, but rather an object that looked like a *Flying Saucer.* A hexagonal-shaped appendage retracted into the underside of the main body, and a number of lights on the appendage flashed, in sequence, green, yellow and red.

Once airborne, the object appeared to be transparent rather than aluminium-coloured, and Dona Maria Nazare said she clearly saw two entities sitting inside. There was little traffic noise from the road at that time, but the witnesses could hear no sound from the object.

On the sea, where the UFO had originally rested, the witnesses saw a white hoop-shaped object "about the size of a truck or jet," according to Dona Maria Nazare. Suddenly, the hoop sank, then it reappeared and a yellow over-shaped section separated from it. This, it was estimated, was some 40 cm across with about 20 cm projecting above the surface of the water. It remained stationary for about three minutes then began to move towards the shore, with its longer axis directed at the witnesses. A green flame at the rear of the object separated from the main body and followed it at a distance of about a metre. After 15 minutes, the yellow oval was about 130 m from the shore, when it made a right-angled turn to itself and headed for the beach at Gavea— a movement directly opposed to the maritime current in the area at the time.

The white hoop disappeared several times, but when it came back into view it was still pursuing its direct course for Gavea Beach, as though it were going to link up once again with the yellow object.

Meanwhile, the police launch Fort Copacabana had arrived at the spot where the UFO had remained stationary, having come to view about 20 minutes after Joao Aguiar made his telephone call. So it seems likely that the crew must has seen the UFO take off. At roughly the position where the hoop had been left, the launch stopped and the police hauled on board a red cylindrical object. They then made off at speed towards their base.

The police made no statement regarding what they saw or found. And, although an account of the incident appeared in the newspaper *Diario de Noticias* on June 28, 1970, no other witnesses came forward to confirm the sighting.

51. Ball Lightning

Ball lightning is regarded as a rare natural atmospheric phenomenon, thought by some never to have been photographed, and doubted, even until recently, to exist by scientists working in meteorology. There are still some who deny that there is proof of the existence of ball lightning. If it does exist, then based on the reports of those who claim to have seen it, ball lightning would appear to be glowing spherical energy, generally moving slowly, and igniting on impact or occasionally passing through solid matter.

Since the beginning of the UFO reporting, there has been a tendency to try to pass off all reports as ball lightning and the counter arguments have always produced those cases of extraordinary detail where ball lightning simply would not fit the explanation.

In reality, it is very likely that ball lightning, if it does exist, explains many UFO reports but would nonetheless leave open many others. It is generally well accepted that the questions raised by the UFO phenomenon will not be answered by any simplistic answer.

The Peter Day film is considered by some to be the first capture of ball lightning on film, though that remains a speculation.

More recently, it has been suggested that an even more extraordinary possibility may exist, with a form of ball lightning actually harbouring intelligence capable of reacting with the human observers. Many of the lights observed in the valleys of Norway, seem to exhibit some of these features.

A further interesting variation on the theory that has been offered is that ball lightning is 'charged' in such a way that it can interfere with the electrical impulses in the brain and cause hallucination. This, it has been argued, could explain even the more exotic UFO sighting; though this still remains highly speculative.

52. Unidentified Clicking Object

An off-duty policeman, Ernst W. Akergerg and his wife, Karin, were leaving their summer cottage on the island of Gotland, Sweden, on the evening of August 5, 1957. Then they both saw a disk-shaped object heading in their direction from the sea. When the UFO reached the shore, several hundred metres away, it made a sharp turn, tilted on its edge and swayed for a few moments. The disk then continued on for about a kilometre, made another sharp turn, and flew out of view.

Almost immediately, another object approached from the same direction and executed the same manoeuvers, both objects made the water ripple and the treetops swayed as they passed at a height of some 60 metres. The Akergbergs estimated the width of the objects to be about 8 metres. They had the shape of a streamlined "bicycle bell" and were of metallic silver-grey colour. Riveted joints could be seen on the bottom. The upper section seemed to rotate slowly over the lower part. Both of the disks had a glowing "cherry-red tube," and their edges had a "fuzzy, glimmering shine." The objects made a repeated "clicking" noise much like the sound made by winding an alarm clock.

After investigating this sighting, the Swedish Air Force classified the objects as "Unidentified."

53. A UFO Cruised Besides a Steamship

There is a curious entry in the logbook of the captain of the *Llandovery Castle. It* tells how, on the night of July 1, 1947, the steamship cruised briefly through the Straits of Madagascar with a UFO.

It was about 11:00 p.m when some of the passengers first noted a bright light travelling overhead. As the light passed over the ship, it lost altitude and speed and began to descent within 15 m of the water. The light was cast downwards at first, creating a search beam that reflected off the water. But then the light went out, and the passengers and crew could see the object beside them.

The witnesses described the craft as gigantic (at least 300 m long), cylindrical, and metallic. Some said it was shaped like a mammoth steel cigar with its end clipped. About five times as long as it was wide, the thing had no visible window or portholes. But because the mysterious craft matched the speed of the *Llandovery Castle* exactly, the crew deduced that something intelligent must be guiding it.

After cruising beside the *Llandovery Castle* for about a minute, the enormous object rose silently. When it was about 300 m in the air, it emitted streams of orange flames and shot upwards, disappearing into the night skies.

54. They can be Devastating Too!

Although rarely violent, the UFOs can sometimes be devastating. On the night of December 13, 1990, the Soviet radar station at Kuybyshev picked up a large blip approaching them at high speed. Two-and-a-half minutes later, the blip broke into many small traces, all maintaining a course that took them to the station.

A unit of soldiers was sent to investigate. They saw a large, black, triangular UFO with smooth sides, about 13.5 m long. The craft was approaching one of the base's radar masts. As it hovered before it, there was a flash and the mast burst into flames.

The object stayed hovering in the sky around the base for over 90 minutes, while the mast burnt and finally crashed to the ground. Later investigation showed that the steel from which the mast was constructed had completely melted.

55. UFO Military Police

Perhaps the strangest wrinkle in the already perplexing UFO phenomenon are the semidemonic figures known as *MIB, or Men in Black.* The first MIB report in modern Ufology came from Albert K. Bender, a teenage UFO buff who directed the International Flying Saucer Bureau and published the bureau's news bulletin, *Space Review.* In September 1953, Bender claimed three men clad in black suits approached him, and told him he must abandon his UFO research if he wanted to stay safe. Bender did indeed abandon his career in Ufology, but the MIB phenomenon went on. The UFO investigator and author, John Keel, for instance, has talked to numerous eyewitnesses who claimed to have been confronted by similar MIB entities.

Some unusual aspects of the MIB phenomenon emerged when the folklorist, Peter Rojcewicz, studied the reports. For instance, Rojcewicz notes, MIB "often dress in black clothing that may appear soiled and generally unkempt or unrealistically neat and wrinkle-free. On occasions, they display a very unusual walking motion, moving about as if their hips were on swivel joints, their torso and legs at odds with one another. Some display a penchant for black Cadillacs or other large, dark sedans. Some MIB show an unusual growth of hair, suggesting that their hair had grown back unevenly after having recently been shaved." Nearly all races and complexions, he says, have been reported with Asian features predominating.

The motives of MIB remain murky. They are frequently bent on retrieving the UFO data and warning witnesses away from any further involvement with the subject. "They may show up at the home or workplace," says Rojcewicz, "demanding photographs or negatives of the UFOs before the witness has even let it be known publicly that he possesses any." On several such occasions, the MIB posed as military intelligence officers.

Where MIBs come from and where they disappear to after their mischief is accomplished, is an enigma. What is known, however, is that their presence further clouds the waters already made murky by the UFO.

56. Detailed Examination failed

In July 1969, representatives of the Aerial Phenomena Research Organisation (APRO) received information about a startling UFO incident that had taken place on a farm near Anolaima, some 64 km from Bogota, Colombia. They made a particularly careful investigation of the case, as one of the witnesses, Arcesio Bermudez, had died eight days after the sighting.

On the evening of July 4, Bermudez and some of his family and friends – five adults and four children in all – were talking inside the farmhouse when they heard shouts from a 13-year-old Mauricio Gnecco, who was outside with another child, Enriquie Osorio. The group went outside and saw yellow-orange light moving across the sky about 180 m away. Mauricio began signalling to the object with a flashlight and it immediately increased its speed and approached the house. It stopped about 50 m away and hovered between two tall trees for about five seconds. It made no sound whatsoever. The witness estimated the height of the object as between 1.2 and 1.8 m and said that it seemed to have an 'arc of light' surrounding it, and two blue luminous legs with green tips.

When the object again began to move, Arcesio Bermudez ran towards it, taking with him Mauricio's flashlight. Mauricio and one of the other children watched from a nearby hill and reported that the object "blinked on and off," then rose in the sky and moved off in the direction of Bogota.

Bermudez returned to the farmhouse and described what he had seen to the others. He said that he had been within 6m of the object, which had "blinked off" and he had seen a "person" inside. From the waist down the person seemed to be shaped like a letter A and was luminous, but otherwise, Bermudez thought it was "normal". Then the object "blinked on", rose into the sky and simply disappeared.

A few minutes later, the object – or another identical one – was seen travelling slowly across the sky at a height of about 90 metres. At approximately the same time, two other people, Clemente Bolivar and Rosalba Prieto, who live 3 km from the farmhouse, also saw a bright orange yellow light moving slowly towards Bogota.

Two days after the sighting, Arcesio Bermudez was taken ill. According to the APRO researcher's report, "his temperature droped to 95° F, and he had a "cold touch" although he claimed he did not feel cold. Within a few days, his condition became far more serious; he had "black vomit" and diarrhoea with blood flow." He was taken to Bogota where, on July 12, he was attended first by Dr Luis Borda and later by Dr. Cesar Esmeal. Neither of them knew of his UFO sighting. However, just before midnight, Arcesio Bermudez died, the cause of death being diagnosed as gastro-enteritis.

Four days later, John Simhon of APRO interviewed the surviving witnesses and invited the children to make drawings of what they had seen. At 8 p.m on the same day, Dr Luis E. Martinez of the National University of Colombia placed four children in a hypnotic trance to see if more details of their experience would be revealed. Their accounts tallied almost exactly with the earlier statements and with those given by the adult witnesses. Also while under hypnosis, the children drew pictures of the 'flying saucer' and these were much the same as the previous drawings.

On July 17, Simhon and Elias Nessim accompanied the witnesses to the scene of the sighting, but no physical evidence of the UFO was found. Further questioning revealed that only Bermudez had claimed to have seen the object land. One of the other witnesses, Luis Carbajal, said that he had heard Bermudez calling him to go and see the object, but stated that he had only seen it flying away between the trees. The investigators pointed out that the farmhouse lies on an air route to Bogota International Airport and suggested that the object could have been a conventional aircraft. However, all the witnesses stated that what they had seen was definitely not an aeroplane.

Simhon then sent details of Bermudez's illness, together with his clothes and wrist watch, to the Colombian Institute of Nuclear Affairs.The symptoms seemed similar to those caused by gama rays.

Other specialists were also provided with details of the Bermudez case. Dr Horace C. Dudley, professor of radiation physics at the University of Illinois Medical Centre in Chicago, stated: "The illness and death of Mr Bermudez may be due to radiation effects. But there is not one bit of laboratory data to support such a conclusion. Without a complete autopsy and pathological study a physician, it would not be warranted in giving a more specific cause of the death."

The APRO consultant in medicine, Dr Benjamin Sawyer, reported: "The symptoms of enteritis are nearly identical to one of the three basic forms of (intestinal) illness from radiation exposure. There is nothing superficially apparent to distinguish the two illnesses." But again, there was insufficient evidence to determine whether the death was due to enteritis or radiation poisoning. Attempts were made to exhume Bermudez's body for detailed examination, but these failed, owing to bureaucratic problems.

57. It Paced B-29 Bomber in India

On August 10, 1944, Captain Alvah M. Reida was piloting a B-29 bomber based at Kharagpur, India, on a mission over Palembang, Sumatra. Then his right gunner and co-pilot noticed a sphere 'probably '1.5-1.8 m to 5m in diameter, of a very bright and intense red or orange in colour' that constantly throbbed, about 3750 m off the starboard wing. It paced the B-29, then flying at a speed of 340 km/h at 4200 m. Reida jinxed his plane to shake it off, but it stayed in the same relative position. After eight minutes, it 'made an abrupt 90° turn and accelerated rapidly, disappearing in the overcast sky.'

58. Condon Committee/ Condono Report

In 1966, Senator Gerald Ford (later President of the United States) initiated the move for a scientific investigation of the UFOs by a government-appointed committee, which later on, was called the *Condon Committee.* Dr Edward Uhler Condon led a team of scientists at Colorado University for a two-year study of the UFO phenomenon.

In December 1968, the committee concluded its findings and published the *Condon Report* which broadly concluded that the UFOs were not of significance for scientific study. However, there is some doubt as to Dr Condon's impartiality in respect of this conclusion. In any case, it appears clear that the conclusions of the report do not necessarily mirror the actual findings of the investigation. In short, the investigation seems to have revealed that there was something of significance to study, but the conclusion published was what the government insisted on.

The Air Force drew the following conclusions from the Condon Report. ' The report concluded that little if anything had come from the study of the UFOs in the past twenty-one years that has added to scientific knowledge'. 'The panel concurred with the University of Colorado's recommendation that no high priority in the UFO investigation is warranted by data of the past two decades.'

59. Stolen UFO Film

Two radar operators from the White Sands Missile Range, New Mexico, picked up a fast-moving unidentified object on the morning of July 14, 1951. A tracer on the ground, who happened to be watching a B-29 with binoculars, saw a large UFO near the plane.

A second ground observer with a 35 mm camera shot 60 metre of film of the object. According to the reports, the film showed a round, bright spot, but the film somehow disappeared and has never been seen since.

60. The Saucer Visited Washington, D.C.

On late Saturday evening, July 19, 1952, seven strange spots suddenly appeared on a radarscope at the Washington National Airport. Unable to identify the blips, air traffic controller, Edward Nugent, asked his supervisor, Harry G. Barnes, to take a look. The following is an excerpt from the report later made by Barnes:

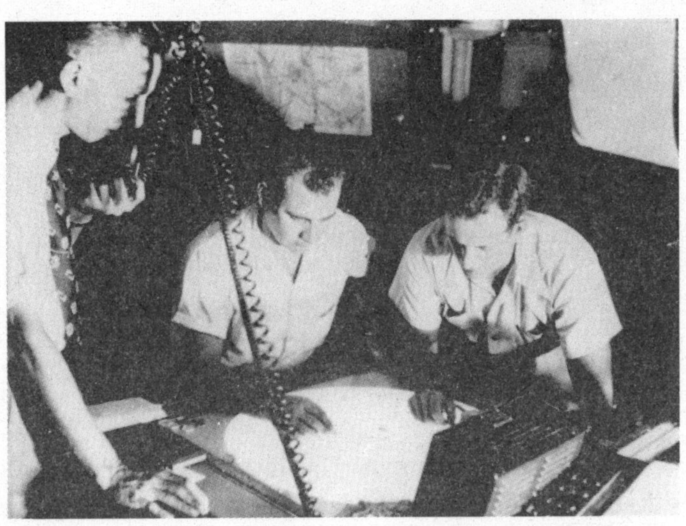

"The things, which caused Ed to call me over to the scope, were seven pips [blips] clustered together irregularly in one corner … the pips showed up as pale violet spots…. The seven pips indicated that the objects were in the air over an area about 14 km in diameter, 24 km south-southwest of Washington. We knew immediately that a very strange situation existed…. We tracked the seven pips for about 5 minutes and quickly determined that they were moving between 160 and

210 km/h, while we could observe them. But their movements were completely radical compared to those of an ordinary aircraft. They followed no set course, were not in any *formation* and we only seemed to be able to track them for about five km at a time....

Barnes instructed the air force to dispatch jet fighters and then continued to watch the radar screen. By now some of the incoming pilots were radioing in that they could see unidentified lights in the sky. Andrews Air Force Base also began to pick up strange signals on its radarscopes. The Washington National Ground personnel also saw a "bright orange light." A commercial airline pilot reported receiving visual images, one of which included six lights. Each light corresponds to a radar blip. Several hours after Barnes's call, jet fighters finally arrived, but they could find nothing. The strange blips were no longer seen on the radar screen. But as soon as the fighters left, the radar targets again appeared on the airport screens. Both visual and coincident radar reports continued through the night.

Exactly a week later, on Saturday, July 26, a similar series of mysterious blips was seen on the airport's radar screen and was confirmed visually by numerous aircrafts. This time jet interceptors arrived quickly, but only one pilot saw anything. He attempted to close with four lights in the distance but failed.

The incident was played up in newspaper headlines across the country. One of them ran: " The Day the Saucers Visited Washington, DC." The air force investigator, however, concluded that both the incidents "were due to mirage effects created by a double-temperature inversion." This conclusion, was denied by Dr. James E. McDonald, a University of Arizona meteorologist who had later conducted his own investigation.

61. Astronomers and the UFO

When a "flying saucer" is spotted by a couple of teenagers or a tired truck driver, it's easy to brush off the incident as a case of overactive imagination. But when three highly trained astronomers spy a UFO at the same time, that's a different story.

On May 30, 1963, the headlines of the *Melbourne Herald* in Australia declared: "Three Astronomers See Flying Saucer." The article itself noted that the incident was "the best authenticated so far." Professor Bart Bok, a world-renowned authority on the Milky Way; Dr. H. Gollonow, a senior astronomer at the Mount Stromi Observatory; and assistant astronomer, Miss M. Mowat, the newspaper reported, had spotted a glowing, reddish orange object around 6:58 p.m, almost directly over the observatory.

The three astronomers tracked the object for one minute as it travelled west to east below the clouds at speeds far too fast to be a balloon. The observers also ruled out a meteor, since the UFO moved slower than those celestial bodies and left no visible trail.

Since the thing was moving under cloud cover, it was far too low to be a satellite, the astronomers reasoned. Besides, a check of satellite charts indicated that none was over the area where the UFO was seen. The Civilian Aviation Control Centre also confirmed that there were no planes in the vicinity at the time.

The three scientists concluded that the object, which they noted, was self-luminous and did not reflect sunlight. It " was definitely man-made!" But what sort of "man"- made this flying craft, or satellite or an aeroplane it was, has never been explained.

62. The Story of the RB-47

Radar sighting of July 17, 1957. This is how it is summarised in the introduction of a long and detailed account of the incident in *Astornoutics & Aeronautics* magazine published by the UFO subcommittee of the American Institute of Aeronautics and Astronautics:

"On July 17, 1957 an Air Force RB-47, equipped with Electronic Countermeasures (ECM) gear and manned by six officers, was followed by an unidentified object for a distance of well over 110 km and for a time period of 1.5 hours.

It was flying from Mississippi, through Louisiana and Texas and into Oklahoma. The cockpit crew saw the object visually at various times as an intensely luminous light, followed by a ground-radar and detected on ECM monitoring gear aboard the RB-47. Of special interest in this case are several instances of simultaneous appearances and disappearances of all the three of those physically distinct "channels," and the rapidity of manoeuvers beyond the prior experience of the aircrew.

The full report runs for five pages in the magazine, listing all the details of the radar and visual observations. The repeated sightings, coinciding with unidentified radar blips, consisted of an "intense white light" that seemed to be "following" the aircraft at times. Attempts to intercept the UFO failed.

Project Blue Book finally dismissed the case by identifying the UFO as American Airlines Flight 655—a completely unfounded conclusion according to many experts, including the officers of the RB-47.

63. They Are Already Here

Many people in Spain believe that aliens from space are already living on Earth. For more than 30 years, a group, who call themselves as *Ummo,* have been sending papers through the post and holding late-night telephone conversations with people all over the country. They allege that they landed from a spacecraft in France in 1950 to help mankind reach maturity. They claim to come from the planet of *Ummo,* which, they say, orbits the star known on the earth maps of the universe as *Wolf 424.*

All communications from *Ummo* have a thumbprint seal with a curious symbol, three horizontal lines crossing one vertical line. In May 1967, members of a Spanish space flight discussion group received invitations bearing the symbol. They were to gather on June 1 at a cafe in Santa Monica, near Madrid, for the evidence of Ummo's existence.

They were at the appointed time, and. sure enough, an object looking like a flying saucer arrived. It had the *Ummo* symbol on its underside. It performed aerial antics over the

Madrid suburb of San Jose de Valderas before landing briefly in view of the cafe.

Many witnesses took photographs of the strange craft before it flew away again. No one has since been able to trace an *Ummo* to find out whether they are really aliens or just very clever hoaxes.

64. Wingless Aircraft

On July 24, 1948 two Eastern Airlines pilots, Clarence S. Chiles and John B. Whitted, 32 km west of Montgomery Alabama, saw an aircraft streaking towards them and thought that it was a jet fighter:

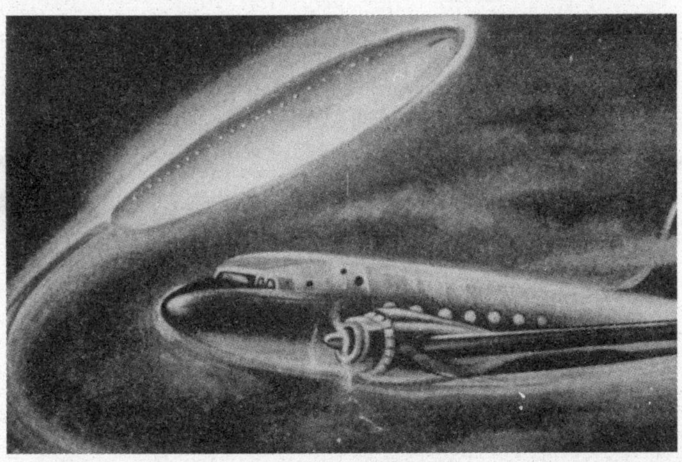

"It was heading southwest, exactly opposite our course. Whatever it was, it flashed down towards us with terrific speed. We veered to the left. It veered sharply, too, and passed us about 170 m to the right. I saw, then it had no wings."

Such was Chiles's report. The mysterious craft passed on Whitted's side, so it was he who had the better view of it. According to him:

"It was about 30 m long, cigar-shaped and wingless, about twice the diameter of a B-29 with no protruding fins". Officer Chiles added to the description:

"An intense dark blue glow came from the side of the ship and ran the entire length of the fuselage like a blue fluorescent light. The exhaust was a red-orange flame...."

Both noticed rows of windows, and a brilliant light inside the object. Chiles also observed a "snout" protruding like a radar pole from the front of the craft. As the UFO passed, it pulled into some broken clouds and was lost from view.

Chiles then visited the cabin to check the passengers. Clarence McKelvie was the only one awake. He too had seen a brilliant flash of light pass by the window. "It looked like a cigar with a cherry flame going out the back. There was a row of windows.... It disappeared very quickly," McKelvie said. The air force investigators, unable to identify the craft, eventually called it a meteor and closed the case.

65. An Unusual Sight

On September 7, 1954 around 7:15 a.m, some 110 km north of Paris, two masons came upon an unusual sight. Emile Renard and Yves Degillerboz were bicycling to work when they had to stop to fix a flat tire. Their attention was attracted by an odd-looking haystack, some 200 m away in a field. It looked as though it was "unfinished," with an "upside-down plate on top."

Then, to their amazement, the "haystack" began to swing back and forth and oscillate slowly. As the masons dropped their bicycles and ran towards it, the object took off at a slant, moving diagonally upward for about 15 m and then flying straight up. They watched the UFO for about three minutes before it disappeared in the clouds. Renard recalled:

"The object flew without making any noise, letting out a little smoke underneath, at the right. It was of bluish-gray colour, and might have been about 9 m in diameter and about 3 m high. As I said before, it looked like a dish turned upside down. On the left side of the bottom, we could see a sort of plate, like a door, wider than it was high. It was about 150 m away from us when it took to the air…."

The masons told their story to a local constable, who much against their will made them repeat their experience to the police in the neighbouring town.

On the same day, from villages scattered over an area of 29 km in the vicinity of this encounter, many people sent in reports of seeing an object corresponding in all details of time, dimensions and colour with the masons' report.

66. Misinterpretations of Objects

On April 17, 1966 a brightly lit object, as big as a house, appeared in the sky of Ravenna, Ohio. Four policemen chased this object for at least an hour or so. The first policeman involved were deputy sheriff Dale Spaur and his assistant, Wilbur Neff, who just before daybreak saw the object coming towards them low over the woods. The UFO was so bright that they were forced to look down. As it hovered overhead, making a humming sound, the two policemen went into their car for protection. Finally, the UFO moved off and Spaur called the headquarters to report the incident. He was told to pursue the object. It was flying slowly, heading into Pennsylvania. Spaur and Neff chased it for some 64 km, when they met Officer Wayne Huston, who also had the object in view. He watched the UFO pass overhead and joined in pursuit. The following is an excerpt from Officer Hustons's report:

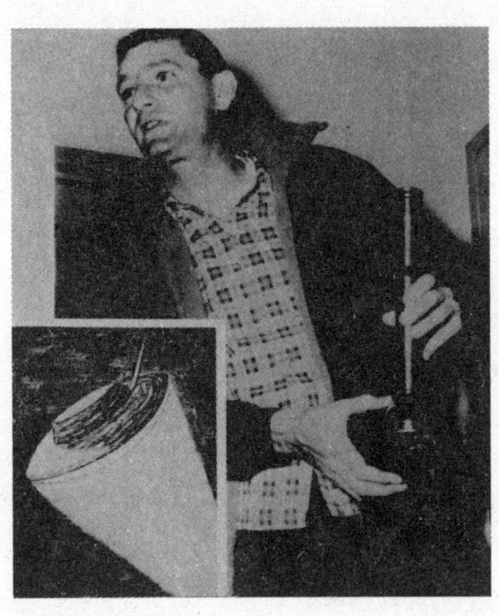

"I watched it go right overhead. As near as I can describe it, it was shaped something like an ice-cream cone. The point of the cone was underneath; the top was like a dome. Spaur and Neff came down the road right after it. I fell in behind them. We were going at 130 to 140 km an hour.... It was right straight ahead...."

The two cars raced on for another 64 km when they saw another police car parked by the road. Officer Frank Panzanell, standing by his car, was watching the UFO in utter amazement. He later said he had been observing the object for about 10 minutes:

"It was very bright and about 7.5 to 9 m in diameter. The object then moved out ... and went straight up real fast to about 1,225 metres ... It continued to go upward until it got as small as a ballpoint pen.... We all four watched the object shoot straight up and disappear...."

The four officers' sworn statements matched in all details. Just before the UFO disappeared, each saw a plane from the Pittsburgh airport pass below it.

After a lengthy investigation, the U.S. Air Force dismissed the sighting as "misinterpretations of conventional objects and natural phenomena"—an unlikely explanation in view of the sequence of events.

67. A Startling Encounter

On September 5, 1980 a road near Gdansk, Poland, was the scene of a startling encounter with a UFO. At about 3.30 a.m, an ambulance with Dr. Barbara Piazza, a driver and a stretcher bearer on board, was rushing Mrs. Elizbieta Pluta, who was in labour, to the local hospital. Suddenly, Dr. Piazza noticed a big red ball in the sky. She asked what it might be, and they all joked about its being a UFO. The ball grew larger until it was about the size of the moon, which was then visible. Soon the UFO was at the level of the treetops and some 180 m away. The driver accelerated, but the object, as the doctor said, "was under intelligent control. We just could not lose it. It was racing after us!" The red ball suddenly appeared about 200 m ahead of the ambulance and blocked the way. Its edges were overlapping the 6 m wide roadway by a half-metre on each side.

Everyone saw the curved bands on the surface, the irregular black lines going up and down in each direction, and the yellow-orange patches on the crimson exterior. Two guards at the nearby railroad crossing were also looking at the UFO. Mrs. Pluta's contractions were now coming in short intervals. The doctor radioed the police, reporting a "UFO" blocking the way." In desperation, she told the driver to flash his headlights. He flashed them twice. Then, at one moment, they saw the UFO right in front of them and the next moment, it vanished "like a TV set when switched off." The ambulance reached the hospital 10 minutes later, and Mrs., Pluta gave birth to a healthy two-and-half kg girl.

68. Saucerport

If the extraterrestrial decide to make their presence known on earth, they may choose to land at areas built by the UFO enthusiasts, especially for visitors from outer space.

In 1973, a retired marine officer drew up plans for some fake flying saucers that could be used as decoys to lure alien pilots. His funds ran out, but in the 1980s, a group called the New Age Foundation was able to create a similar landing strip designed to attract the UFOs. The group christened the 6 hectare site, near Mount Rainier in Washington state, Spaceport Earth.

Farther south, in Lawson Valley, near San Diego, California, the UFO buffs have constructed another saucerport. Ruth Norman, head of the Unarius Education Foundation, who believes extraterrestrial will soon be parking their spacecraft in the area, owns it.

69. The Florida Skymaster

On the night of August 19, 1952, Mr. C. S. Desverges was driving three scouts home when he noticed a light just above a palmetto thicket. The scoutmaster stopped the car, told the boys to go for assistance if he did not return in 15 minutes, and went ahead on foot with a flashlight to investigate what he thought might be a small aircraft making an emergency landing. According to the statement, Desverges later made to a sheriff and air force officials. He became aware of a pungent odour and felt a sudden rise in temperature after hacking his way into the thicket with a machete to the spot where he thought he had seen the light. He continued on for about 9 m into a clearing. Here the heat became almost unbearable. When he looked up at the sky to get his bearings, a dark shape overhead totally obscured his view. He backed away and shone his flashlight at the object, which was hovering 9 to 12 m above the ground. It was disk shaped, with a smooth and gray surface. The underpart was concave, and the upper portion had a dome in the centre. Along the edges of the object were vanes with small openings in between. Then he heard a sound, "like the opening of a well-oiled safe door," and a small red ball that expanded into a red, misty cloud drifted towards him. As the mist closed in, he fainted.

The three boys had been watching their scoutmaster's progress through the thicket by the light of his flashlight. After 10 minutes, they said in their later statements, they could see him shine his flashlight upward; then a red ball of fire enveloped him and they saw him fall. They got out of the car and ran to a neighbouring farmhouse for help.

By the time, the deputy sheriff and a constable arrived, Desverges had recovered consciousness and was stumbling back onto the road. He told his story in a coherent manner and everyone went back to the clearing, but other than finding Desverges's flashlight and machete on the ground, and some flattened grass, nothing out of the ordinary was visible. It was only later, driving back in the car, that Desverges noticed that the hair on his arm was singed and that there were slight burns on his arms and hands; his cap was also slightly charred.

Desverges's injuries remained unexplained, however, as did the tiny holes and scorch marks, which appeared to have been made by electrical sparks, on his cap.

70. Ezekiel and UFO

Josef F. Blumrich, a NASA space engineer who had spent most of his time designing and building aircraft and rockets, including the giant Saturn V rocket, was irritated with Erich Von Daniken's idea that what the prophet Ezekiel had seen was a UFO, and set out to refute him.

Incredibly, he himself became a convert, and worked out reconstruction of the spacecraft he thought Ezekiel had seen, including details of how it might have been operated.

71. Sighting of UFO Occupants

The first sighting of the UFO occupants to be reported after the Arnold case happened on July 23, 1947, near Bauru, Brazil. Jose' Higgins, working on a survey crew, heard a piercing high-pitched whistle just before he saw a large disk-shaped object land. He estimated it to be 45 m in diameter. It seemed to be made of grayish-white metal with a distinct three-foot-wide rim around it.

The object was resting on curved legs. The other members of the crew all fled, and Higgins found himself alone with three entities, each 2 m tall. They wore "rubber-like bags" and had " metal boxes" on their backs. Their clothing, which could be seen through the outer suits, resembled coloured paper.

The occupants all looked alike. They had huge round eyes and large round bald heads without eyebrows or beards. Their bodies were similar to ours except that the legs were longer in proportion. They seemed very beautiful in a sexless kind of way to Higgins.

One of them used a stick to make eight holes in the ground that suggested a solar system with seven planets. He pointed to the outermost one as being their home and called it Orque. (Some UFO buffs interpret this to mean that they came from Uranus.)

They tried to lure Higgins into their craft, but he managed to get away. Hiding for about 30 minutes in a thicket, he watched them leaping and gambolling, playfully throwing huge stones about. Then they boarded the disk, which took off and disappeared towards the north.

72. Extraterrestrial Buried on Earth

On April 19, 1897, something so extraordinary happened in the tiny farming community of Aurora, Texas, that townsfolk talk about it still. According to accounts published in the *Dallas* and *Fort Worth* newspapers of the time, on the fateful spring day, a cigar-shaped spaceship roared out of the sky and slammed into Judge J.S. Proctor's home, destroying a window, a water trough and a flower garden in the process.

S. E. Hayden, a local cotton buyer and newspaper correspondent, reported that the little man who piloted the craft was dismembered by the crash. "However, enough remains were picked up to determine it was not an inhabitant of this world," Hayden wrote in a newspaper article describing the strange event. "The men of the community gathered it up, and it was given a Christian burial in the Aurora cemetery."

The alien's grave marker disappeared several years ago. Residents of Aurora claim they are no longer sure where the grave is and they doubt much could remain in it. But, periodically, areas of the cemetery are dug up, most likely by people hoping to find the remains of the only extraterrestrial being said to have be buried on the planet Earth.

73. UFO 'Mother Ship'

A fleet of four Portuguese jet fighter-bombers under the command of Capt. Jose Louis Ferreira had an encounter with a UFO "mother ship": and its attendant "satellites." The planes were flying at 7,500 m between Granada, Spain, and Portalegre, Portugal, on the night of September 4, 1957, when the captain noticed an object resembling a very bright star, "unusually big and scintillating with a coloured nucleus which changed colour constantly, going from deep green to blue. The other pilots also saw the object.

Suddenly, the UFO appeared to enlarge, growing to five or six times its original size. Then the object seemed to shrink to a barely visible yellow point. These expansions and contractions were repeated several times, Captain Ferreira thought that these changes in size might have been due to shifts in positions.

The bombers now changed their line of flight, but the object maintained its position at 90 degrees to their left. The UFO was now bright red. Suddenly, the pilots noticed a small circle of yellow light emerging from it. They then saw three other similar yellow objects to the right of the main UFO. After further manoeuvers, the small objects began to disappear.

All the pilots agreed that what they had witnessed had no rational explanation. Speaking for everyone, Captain Ferriera stated: "After this please do not give us the old routine of Venus, balloons, aircraft and the like which have been given as a general panacea for almost every case of the UFOs."

74. Cutty Sark Award

Kenneth Arnold, an experienced pilot, flying his plane over the Cascade Mountains of Washington in 1947, suddenly saw nine unidentified circular metal objects flying at an estimated speed of 2080 km/h. Since then, thousands of UFO sightings have been reported over the plains, mountains, desert, lakes, oceans, and cities of Earth. Although strange objects have been noted in the skies through the centuries, the Arnold sighting seemed to launch an avalanche of reports, which has continued ever since.

Though many UFOs have been photographed, not one has been produced for public inspection. Their landing tracks on the Earth have been tested for traces of minerals or chemicals, for geometric signs or mathematical indications. Also their flight and takeoff patterns have been compared with other international reports.

According to the *People's Almanac* (Bantam, 1981), the Cutty Sark Company of 3 St. James Street, London SW1, has posted a bonafide reward of £1,000,000 to anyone able to capture a "spaceship or other vehicle" that is verified by the Science Museum of London as having "come from outer space." The Cutty Sark Company, makers of Scotch whisky, claims that the reward for a provable UFO is a serious offer, and the company has taken out insurance to cover the possible expense.

Although no one has yet claimed this prize money, a possible candidate is rumoured to exist in the form of a crashed flying saucer or spaceship found in July 2, 1947, near Socorro, New Mexico "(The Roswell Incident" Ace Books, 1988). The saucerlike spaceship was first taken to Roswell Air Force Base and then shipped for further examination, along with its dead humanoid crew to the Muroc Air Force Base in California for inspection by President Eisenhower and others. They, however, maintained military security with the press.

After that, it was sent to Wright-Patterson Air Force Base, Ohio, where it was held in Building 18A, Area B. Eventually, it was sent to Langley Field, Virginia, headquarters of the CIA. Other parts of the wreck are rumoured to be at McDill Air Force Base in Florida, and photographs are alleged to be on file or exhibit in the "Blue Room" at Wright-Patterson, where a top-secret exhibit of the UFO activity is displayed.

It is unlikely that Cutty Sark will have to make good the reward in the case of the Roswell incident because all corroborative reports concerning it were now classified. Nevertheless, when the incident first occurred, the press gave it a wide coverage in interviews with civilians as well as military personnel.

These reports, however, do not qualify for the Cutty Sark award. Cutty Sark will keep its £1,000,000, and its whisky label will continue to feature a sailing ship and not an interplanetary spacecraft, if there is any concrete proof of captured secret. During the present world situation, knowledge of the construction and operation of UFOs from space or from Earth itself would represent an extraordinary advantage to the country possessing it.

75. Honest Housewives

In May 1981, the British UFO Research Association launched a major investigation in the Scottish border regions after two women reported a series of strange sightings.

Mrs Mary Watson and Mrs Joyce Byers, both of Moffat, Dumfries, said they had logged more than 100 separate UFO sightings in a diary provided by Eskdalemuir Observatory. "We have noted everything from swirling, saucer-shaped objects to orange and red triangles," said Mrs Byers.

The women said they believed the Moffat Hills might be a base for the UFOs, and that there could be a link with a series of mysterious plane crashes in the border country, in which 12 people had died. They also pointed out that two nuclear power stations, Chapelcross and Windscale, were within an easy flying distance.

Stuart Campbell of UFO Research Association said: "Inquiries are being made. The two women are not the sort to make up stories."

76. Film Footage of a UFO

During the 1972 filming of a television commercial on the roof of San Juan's Hotel Sheraton in Puerto Rico, the crew witnessed the sudden approach of a large UFO. Viewing it on the monitors, they could tell that the brightly glowing object was neither a plane, nor a helicopter. It vanished as quickly as it had appeared, but not before it ruined the commercial, which had to be reshot.

That year, there were more reports of the UFOs (unidentified flying objects, not necessarily extraterrestrial in origin) in Puerto Rico than anywhere else in the world. So the Sheraton was no exception. The film footage of the large, glowing UFO was sold to Creative Films, a movie company that needed a shot of a UFO in a film it was making at the time.

77. Mystery Remains Unsolved

The closing months of 1978 marked some very unusual UFO-associated events for the Australian sector of the globe. The tragic case of Frederick Valentich is the starting point of a whole series of visual, radar and filmed recordings of bizarre flying objects.

"It is approaching from due east of me," radioed the young Australian pilot, 50 minutes after he had taken off from Moorabbin Airport, Victoria, on a solo flight in a Cessna 183 aircraft across the Bass Strait to King Island. His terse message continued:

"It seems to be playing some sort of game. Flying at speed I cannot estimate....It is flying past. It has a long shape ... coming for me right now.... It has a green light and sort of metallic light on the outside."

Valentich was reporting back to Melbourne air flight service controller Steve Robey, after he had radioed a request for confirmation of a large craft with "four bright lights" and been told that there were no reported aircraft in the area.

"The thing is orbiting on top of me."

The Cessna's engine now began to rough-idle and cough, and Valentich called in to announce:

"Proceeding King Island. Unknown aircraft now hovering on top of me."

With these words, the young pilot signed off. A loud metallic sound was heard at ground reception for 17 seconds, and then communications went dead. No sign of either Valentich or his plane was ever found, and the mystery remains unsolved to this day.

78. A Satellite from Other World

In July 1960, a *Newsweek* article noted that the number of man-made objects known to be orbiting the Earth didn't jibe with the actual number of satellites that had been sent into space. The National Space Surveillance Centre said, the United States had eleven in orbit and the Soviet Union had two.

But according to the *Newsweek* article, several scientists claimed that at least one other spacecraft was circling the planet. Where did it come from?

"This satellite, the scientists suspect, is a visitor sent by the beings of another star within our own Milky Way—a sort of United Stellar Organisation, perhaps—interested, for archaeological reasons, in how things are going in this part of the galactic neighbourhood," *Newsweek* reported.

Could the alien satellite have been the same UFO spotted on December 18, 1957? That evening, around 6:00 p.m, Dr. Luis Corrales of the Communications Ministry in Caracas, Venezuela, snapped a photo of the Soviets' Sputnik II. When Dr. Corrales developed the picture, he was startled to find that he had captured another object on film, too.

Alongside the Russian satellite was a UFO, which showed up as a streak of light because of the short time exposure Dr. Corrales had used.

When researchers examined the photo, they concluded that the object wasn't a meteor or star. Instead, they determined that it was an unrecognisable kind of intelligently controlled craft that was able to deviate from the path of the Sputnik II, and then return to its side.

79. After Effect of Trace Touch

Near Delphos, Kansas, a 16-year-old Ronald Johnson was tending sheep on his father's farm with his dog on the evening of November 2, 1971. Suddenly, he saw a mushroom-shaped object, with multicoloured lights covering its surface. The UFO was only 25 m away, hovering within 2 m of the ground. Ronald estimated its diameter to be about 3 metres. The object sounded much like "an old washing machine which vibrates." Before it took off, an intense light issued from its base, temporarily blinding Ronald. When he regained his sight after a few minutes, he rushed into the house to call his parents. The whole family went outside and they all said they saw the object, "–now high in the sky before it vanished.

At the site, where the UFO had hovered, the three witnesses saw "a glowing ring on the ground" and luminescence on parts of the surrounding trees. One investigator said that the texture of the soil "felt strange, like a slick crust, as if the soil was crystallised." Ronald's mother, a nurse, reported that her fingers felt numb, "as if a local anaesthetic had been applied," after touching the UFO trace. This condition lasted for two weeks. A month later, snow fell and melted on the ground except on the ring, which remained white.

On examination, it was found that the ground beneath the ring was impermeable to water and "dry to a depth of at least 30 cm." Also, a soil sample from the ring area contained a high concentration of a primitive organism of the genus, *Nocardia,* which is often found growing with a fungus that is at times fluorescent. If energy emanating from a UFO had triggered their coincidental growth, this could explain the glowing ring.

Every evening for about two weeks after the event, the sheep would jump out of the pen and run wildly. The dog, too, would desperately try to get into the house at sunset. Ronald was also affected, suffering eye irritation, headaches and recurring nightmares from which he would awaken screaming.

80. The Boomerang Shaped UFO

On several nights from March 17 through March 31, 1983, hundreds of Westchester county, New York, residents witnessed a dazzling sight, like a boomerang-shaped craft, that hovered over them soundlessly, displaying bright rays of light. The multiple reports were unusual, as J. Allen Hynek, Director of the Centre for UFO studies in Evanston, Illinois, pointed out, because most UFO sightings are isolated occurrences. "But this UFO was seen in a relatively urban area over a number of days," he stated, "with a broad spectrum of witnesses."

Meteorologist, Bill Hele, was the first to spot the strange check mark-shaped object with rows of multicoloured lights as he drove downs the Taconic State Parkway.

He saw the lights blink off for a moment; then they came back on this time flashing a brilliant green. Hele reported that the craft, which hovered 300 m in the air for two or three minutes before it drifted out of view to the north, was almost 900 m across.

Within a few days, other sightings were pouring in and the Centre for UFO Studies launched an investigation headed by Westchester science teacher Phil Imbrogno, coinvestigator George Lesnick and Hynek himself. The team interviewed a host of witnesses, including doctors, nurses, lawyers, business executives, housewives, and a group of striking Metro-North trainmen. They also used an Apple II computer to cross match the information they came up with. The results? All the descriptions of the UFO closely matched Hele's.

But the investigators also came up with some contradictions. Since sightings occurred in towns, kilometres apart at the same time, could multiple UFOs have been in the sky? The evidence pointed to that possibility. However, reports of hundreds of sightings in five Connecticut towns, a month after the Westchester incidents seemed to point to a hoax. The witnesses there heard engines and saw manoeuvers that could have been performed by small planes flying in formation.

Nonetheless, the investigators declared this latter event differed substantially from the genuine UFO sightings of a boomerang-shaped craft over New York. Imbrogno stated, "Single-engine planes cannot hover soundlessly, make ninety degree turns, or shoot down dazzling beams of light."

81. No Trace of Dog

Angler Alan Morris claims that a UFO crew kidnapped his dog. Morris, of Bethesda, Wales, told police he was fishing in a river near his home when a ball of pulsating light approached.

"It hovered for a while over where I was sitting, then landed in a nearby field," he said. "I moved closer to get a better look."

Morris said he saw a hatch open in the side of saucer-shaped craft. A metallic-looking ladder dropped down to the ground, and three beings climbed down it. "They were about 2 m tall, with antennae on their heads," he recalled. "They each seemed to be carrying spades and containers."

When the figures started digging, Morris's dog suddenly ran towards them. The fisherman stood up to call him back, then blacked out.

By the time he opened his eyes again, the saucer had vanished, leaving only burn marks on the spot where it had been. And there was no sign of the dog.

82. Near Death Experience

Lorraine Davis, a researcher at John F. Kennedy University in Oriand, California, conducted a study under the university's consciousness studies department. She says the study may show that the UFOs have an explanation most people have overlooked. Instead of being spaceships from other galaxies, they could be psychic phenomena related to the bright lights some people see before they die.

Davis came up with the idea after attending a seminar on the near-death experiences (NDEs) led by the University of Connecticut, psychologist Kenneth Ring. Davis noted striking similarities between the altered state of consciousness described by the near-death survivors, including seeing an almost blinding light and glimpsing long-dead relatives, and the experiences reported by the UFO contactees. Using an NDE questionnaire developed by Ring, Davis contacted 261 people who said they had been in contact with the UFOs.

When she analysed the ninety-three replies she received, Davis found that a remarkable pattern stood out. Like people who had been revived from clinical death, those who had seen a UFO consistently said they, too, had undergone three profound changes. Their attitudes towards themselves and other people became less egocentric, and their personal religious beliefs moved from atheism or sectarianism to a kind of universal spirituality. They also reported that their psychic abilities had notably increased.

Davis thinks that UFO sightings and NDEs are both examples of altered states of human consciousness. "The UFO participant was thrust into this psychic state by a precipitating event," she says, "just as the NDE subject was transformed by the nearness of death."

This does not mean, she emphasises that people who see the UFOs are just imaging the experiences.

"If the UFO experience does take place in an altered state of consciousness, perhaps a nuts-and-bolts machine is materialised for a few minutes," she says. "Who knows? It's certainly possible to perceive and experience in other states of consciousness, sometimes with an even greater sense of reality than that which we experience on a day-to-day basis."

83. Some Interesting Traces

On the night of September 27, 1972, a UFO landed in the Transylvanian Alps, Romania. An elderly night watchman from the parish of Posesti had seen a mysterious object moving through the sky and then settling down on a hillside. The next morning, villagers went to the place where the watchman thought the UFO had landed, and found a cornfield with a clump of cornstalks bent over about a metre from the ground. The patch of bent corn formed a circle about 6 m in diameter, and in the centre of this circle was a narrow, 2.5 m deep cylindrical hole apparently bored into the Earth. Radiating from it were three evenly spaced long rectangular imprints in the soil. The local people received the impressions that a rounded object with three ground supports had dropped down into the cornfield.

An investigating team from Bucharest University arrived a few weeks later. They measured the imprints, photographed the site, studied the topography and took away some 20 samples of soil and vegetation for analysis. The investigators concluded that some very heavy objects had indeed landed, resting on a three-footed pad. Since the corn had not been flattened, it was assumed that the body had been about a metre off the ground. The UFO must have made a vertical landing and taken off between the three apple trees that remained undamaged.

The soil analysis revealed unusual radioactivity and the sample of grass taken from the circle proved to be scorched. It was also found that the biological rhythm of the moles living close by had been disturbed. Although it was only autumn, they were beginning to come out of hibernation, unlike other members of their species farther away from the site.

84. I Need Witnesses

Most people were napping on the overnight flight between Fortaleza and Sao Paulo, Brazil, in February 1982, when pilot Gerson Maciel De Britto made an unexpected announcement: "I see a strange object 64 to 80 km to the left and I need eyewitnesses."

The passengers stirred and discovered that they were bathed in a brilliant light. Looking out of the plane's windows for the next hour and twenty-two minutes, they observed the sky turn red, orange, white, and blue.

From his vantage point in the cockpit, De Britto made out a "fast-moving, saucer-shaped disk with five spotlights." When the objects failed to establish contact after De Britto sent it radio messages in Portuguese and English, he tried communicating through concentration attempting to send or receive information telepathically.

As the airliner approached within 13 km of Rio de Janeiro for a scheduled stopover, the pilot noted that the UFO was only 13 km from the plane and moving closer. Although the radar failed to pick up the object, the Rio tower asked three commercial pilots flying in the area whether they saw the strange light and were told they did. Brazilian military planes were soon soaring after the craft. The official report of the outcome of that chase remains classified.

After major Brazilian newspapers and magazines carried the story, the UFO sceptics began pointing out that Venus had risen in the eastern sky at 3:10 a.m. on the morning in question. Could pilot De Britto and his plane's passengers have been fooled into thinking they saw a UFO by the intense and colourful glow of the planet?

De Britto says that's impossible. He insists he saw Venus and the strange object. In addition, he says that the light maintained the same orientation to the plane even after he changed course by 51 degrees which suggests an intelligent force was manning the craft. "If what the pilot says is true, then it could not have been Venus," noted J. Allen Hynek, director of the Centre for UFO studies in Evanston, Illinois. "If it wasn't Venus, then it was a UFO."

85. Power of Life and Death

Did a flying saucer kill 15 ponies on Dartmoor? Members of the Devon Unidentified Flying Objects Centre believe it did. The dead ponies were found close together in a little valley far away from any of the roads over the moors. Their bones were crushed, their ribs cracked and their flesh had rotten away to leave bare skeletons in only 48 hours, far quicker than normal.

Four UFO investigators took over the case in July 1975 after animal experts declared themselves baffled. They searched the area with geiger counters and metal detectors. Though they found nothing, the group leader, John Wyse, a bandsman in the army, said: "I think the ponies were crushed by the anti-gravity field of a flying saucer as it took off."

A UFO was also the prime suspect when animals died mysteriously in a zoo at Newquay, Cornwall. Three ducks, a goose, a swan and two baby wallabies were found dead on the morning after strange lights were reported over the town. One bird was decapitated. Detectives were said to have discovered that the bodies gave off positive radiation readings.

In Minnesota, top American UFO investigator Dr. J. Allen Hynek was called in after farm animals were found mutilated. There were no human footprints near the bodies, and no signs of attack by predators. Internal organs appeared to have been removed by surgical instruments, and many cows had had their blood sucked out.

Dr Hynek said that 22 cattle were killed during the late 1960s and that curious deaths recurred in 1973 around the towns of Canby, Viking, Warroad and Kimball. He appealed to the farmers to contact him at his UFO Centre in Evanston, Illinois, whenever they found more bodies.

Apart from making life painful for humans – and possibly holding the power of life and death over both men and animals – the UFOs may have the ability to control some of Earth's most sophisticated scientific achievements.

86. Pint-sized Alien

On November 28, 1954, two terrified men burst through the doors of the police station in Caracas, Venezuela. The story they related sounded so farfetched that they were immediately dismissed as drunks. Later on when medical tests showed they were cold, sober and suffering from shock, it was obvious that something very real and very extraordinary had happened to Gustavo Gonzales and Jose' Ponce.

According to their sworn testimonies, the two men left Caracas in a truck around 2:00 a.m. and headed for Petare, a town about twenty minutes down the road. Halfway there, they found a glowing, curved object blocking the highway.

The craft was floating about 1.5 m above the road and Ponce and Gonzales decided to take a closer look. As they approached the object, a small, dark, hairy, manlike creature clad only in a loincloth came towards them. Gonzales quickly grabbed him and was surprised that the "man" weighed very little, probably about 15 kg. But touching the creature proved to be dangerous.

Immediately, Gonzales was thrown about 4.5 metres. Ponce turned and fled towards the police station. As he glanced back, he saw two other small humanoids running towards their luminous ship holding vegetation in their hands.

The police could not easily forget the tale, because it was quickly corroborated by an independent, reliable source. Two days after the men encountered the strange creatures, one of the physician who had examined them came forward. Although, he was hesitant to talk at first because he did not want to be associated with such a strange event, he finally admitted that while driving home from an emergency call, he had witnessed the entire episode. It had happened, he said, just as Gonzales and Ponce had said — the UFO, hairy, pint-sized alien, and all.

87. A Thought-provoking Image

On May 11, 1950, a UFO passed over the Trent farm near McMinnville in Oregon. Mrs Trent was outside feeding rabbits and she noticed a huge disc-shaped object flying towards her.

She called her husband who brought their camera and the Trents were able to take two black and white photographs of the object as it passed silently across the sky.

Even the Condon Committee was forced to list these photographs as the only ones they were unable to dismiss and in their findings concluded that the photographs were consistent with the Trents' description of the UFO. The Condon Report remarked, "This is one of the few UFO reports in which all factors investigated, geometric, psychological and physical, appear to be consistent with the assertion that an extraordinary flying object, silvery, metallic, disc-shaped, tens of metres in diameter, and evidently artificial, flew within sight of two witnesses.

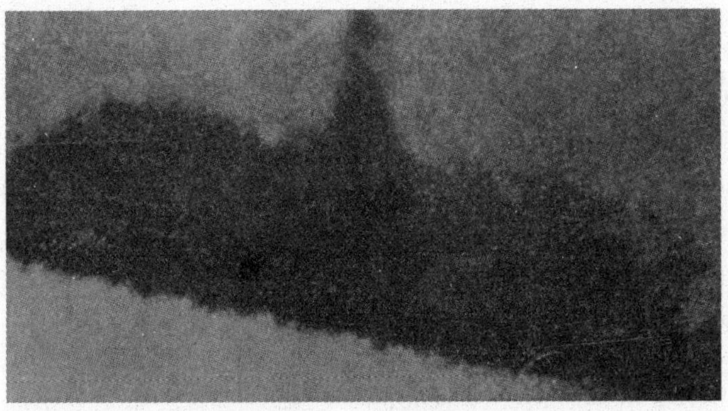

In more modern times, these photographs were subjected to complex computer analysis and they, too, confirm that the object appears to be large and distant. There was no evidence of supporting wires or other clues that the object may have been faked and it, therefore, remains a most thought-provoking image.

The photographs proved to be almost identical to a photograph taken by a pilot in Rouen, France, in the summer of 1954.

88. The Nevada UFO Crash

On April 18, 1962, reports came in that a red object had been seen in the skies over Oneida, New York, heading west. Although the radar picked up the thing, it could not be identified. When it went as far as the Midwest, the Air Defence Command scrambled jets from Phoenix to intercept the UFO.

But when the object was about 120 km Northwest of Las Vegas, it disappeared from the radar screens. According to the *Las Vegas Sun*, the only newspaper that investigated the event, the UFO may have exploded over Nevada. At about the same time, the object vanished from the radar screens, the paper pointed out and an explosion took place somewhere above the Mesquite Range.The blast was so powerful that the streets of Reno became as bright as day. Although many people chalked the brilliant flash up to an atomic bomb test, the Atomic Energy Commission denied that any nuclear tests were underway in the United States at that time.

A few hours later, another strange scenario that may or may not be related was reported by the United Press International. A huge object had been spotted landing near a Eureka, Utah, electric power station. Once again, *Las Vegas Sun* reporters checked out the story, and, when they questioned a Stead Air Force Base official in Reno, they were told that the landing had occurred. The spokesman, who requested anonymity, also commented that the "impact" of the UFO's landing had knocked the power station out of order.

Curiously, few Americans ever heard about the strange objects that rocked the Southwest that spring evening, only the *Las Vegas Sun* and a couple of regional papers ever printed the news that a "flying saucer" had apparently crashed on Earth.

89. An Improbable Coincidence

It is generally assumed that the UFO landings are furtive affairs, conducted in relatively isolated areas, far from prying eyes. No UFO, for example, has ever turned up on the White House lawn, or touched down in Red Square.

Nevertheless, the UFOs are frequently been sighted in populated cities. A number of people claim to have seen one landing in the Stonehenge Apartments, in Jersey City, on the night of January 12, 1975. The spherical object was seen by at least nine observers, including the doorman, both in and outside the apartment building.

According to published reports, after the UFO settled to the ground in the park, a hatch opened, and small humanoid occupants, dressed like "kid in snowsuits," descended a ladder. They then dug around in the grass with what looked to be shovel-like instruments.

After dumping the soil samples into the equivalent of extraterrestrial pails, the tiny humanoids reboarded the UFO. It then lifted off with a bright flash of light and vanished in the night sky. The "dark, almost black" sphere made a droning noise, like a "refrigerator motor."

A year later, in January and February 1976, the UFO seemingly revisited the scene of its earlier excavations. It was seen on three separate occasions by Stonehenge Apartment tenants and pedestrians simply passing by. An improbable coincidence exists in the name of the apartments. For in England, on the Salisbury Plain, the strange and unidentified ruins of Stonehenge have often been supposed to have been constructed by or received visits from the extraterrestrials.

90. UFO in Group

In June 1954, the Stratoliner of the British Overseas Airways Corporation was 5 km out of New York, on its way to London. At this point of time, Captain James H. Howard noticed a large elongated object and six smaller objects about 5 km off on their left side.

As the plane approached Goose Bay, Canada, for re-fuelling, the large UFO seemed to change shape and the smaller ones converged on it. Then they seemed to disappear inside it, and the big one shrank.

Howard contacted the Ground Control and the US airforce sent a Saber Fighter to the scene. Captain Howard did not see what happened, because he had to leave Goose Bay for London.

However, his co-pilot, and several passengers all confirmed the sighting of the UFO. But in 1968, the United States airforce dismissed the sighting as ' an optical mirage phenomenon '.

91. Foo Fighters

Popular history dates the beginning of the modern UFO phenomenon to the summer of 1947. Then Idaho businessman, Kenneth Arnold, saw nine silvery, crescent-shaped objects flying in formation like "a saucer skipping over water" near Mount Rainier, in Washington state. Several years earlier, however, at the height of World War II, similar flying saucers were reported by both Allied and Axis car crews in the European and Pacific campaigns.

On the allied side, at least, such nocturnal lights and daylight disks were known as Foo Fighters. It was after popular Smokey Stover cartoon character, who was forever mumbling, "Where there's foo, there's fire." Foo itself, of course, was a play on the French word, few, for fire.

The best documented Foo Fighter encounter occurred on Bolack Thursday on October 14, 1943 when B-17 Flying Fortresses of the American Eighth Air Force suffered disastrous causalities during a daylight bombing raid on the Scheweinfurt's heavily defended ball bearing factories. Historina Marin Caidin called it "one of the most baffling incidents of World War II, and an enigma that to this day defies explanation."

As the 384th bombardment group completed its run over the target, numerous pilots and top-turret gunners in the staggered formation reported a cluster of small silver disks straight ahead.

Plane number 026, in an effort to avoid a head-on collision, took immediate evasive action, but too late: According to the debriefing report, "the bomber's right wind went directly surface." The pilot did add that one of the disks was heard to strike his tail assembly, but that no explosion or damage followed.

Accompanying the disks at a distance of about 6 m were several clumps of black debris measuring about a square metre in size. This, too, seemed to have no harmful effect on the Flying Fortresses. The debriefing report also noted that two other aircraft flew through the disks with no apparent damage.

Foo Fighters were also seen as nocturnal lights of an orange, red, or white hue. On the night of November 23, 1944, for instance, a three-man crew assigned to the 415th Night Fighter squadron encountered eight to ten of the mysterious globes over the Rhine river, north of Strasbourg. They looked at first like distant twinkling stars, said intelligence officer lieutenant Fred Ringwald, but within minutes appeared as orange balls "moving through the air at a terrific speed."

Another B-17 pilot, Charles Odom of Houston, recalled his daytime Foo Fighter experience after the war. The saucers "looked like crystal balls about the size of basketballs," he said. They seemed to "become magnetised to our formation and fly alongside. After a while, they would peel off like a plane and leave."

92. Bender's Prophecy

Albert K. Bender, who founded the International Flying Saucer Bureau, and disbanded it in 1953, claimed that he had done so after an interview with a 'spaceman,' who warned him that he would be killed if he continued to delve into the mystery of flying saucers.

Seven years later, Bender finally told the story, and also said that he asked the space being whom he called the 'Exalted One,' various questions. Asked if he believed in God, the Exalted One replied that 'they' had no need to believe in things, as the people on Earth did. Asked if there was life on Mars, he said there had been, but the invaders destroyed it. The Martians had built beautiful cities and developed vast canals, but had not been as technologically advanced at the time of their destruction as Earth's civilisation is now. According to the Exalted One, Venus was now developing life.

When Bender asked, if Earth's people would reach the moon, the Exalted One said, 'yes'. Seven years later, the prophecy came true.

93. A Red Light in Pursuit

On the evening of December 12, 1967, Rita Malley, a young mother of two, was driving home to Ithaca, New York. She then noticed a red light in pursuit. At first, she thought a police car was following her. She was about to pull over to the side of the road, when she took another look. This time around, she saw that the light was attached to a strange flying object travelling just above the power lines to her left.

That was startling enough, but it was nothing compared to her sudden realisation that she could no longer control her car. She shouted to her son, who was travelling with her, to brace himself for an accident. But strangely, he did not respond or even move." "It was as if he were in some kind of a trance," she said later.

"The car pulled over to the shoulder of the road by itself, ran over an embankment into an alfalfa field, and stopped."

Malley said, "A white twirling beam of light flashed down from the object, and I heard a humming sound. Then I began to hear voices. The voices were broken and jerky, like the way a translator sounds when he is repeating a speech at the United Nations." As she recalled it, she became hysterical when the voices told her a friend was involved in a terrible accident some kilometers away. After a while, her car began to move again. She pushed down hard on the accelerator and sped home.

"I knew something was wrong when she walked into the house," her husband, John, told a reporter for the *Syracuse Herald-Journal*. "I thought maybe she had had an accident with the car or something." The next day she learnt that a friend, indeed, had experienced a serious car accident, the night before.

According to reporters and the UFO investigators, who interviewed her, for days afterwards, Mrs. Malley could not discuss the bizarre experience without bursting into tears.

94. An Encounter with Iranian Air Force

People in Teheran, Iran, started calling the Iranian Air Force command post at around midnight on September 19, 1976, with reports of a strange object in the sky. The descriptions ranged from "birdlike" and "bright light" to "helicopter with a shining light." B. G. Yousefit, assistant deputy commander of operations, decided to send up an F-4 jet from Shahrokhi air force base to investigate, and possibly intercept the UFO. This plane, however, lost all communications instrumentation about 64 km along its intercepting path. The pilot headed back, and another F-4 was sent up.

As this second plane approached the UFO, radar contact was made. The radar return was reported to be about what would be expected from a Boeing 707 aircraft. When the second F-4 reached the point at which the first jet had lost its communications, the UFO suddenly increased its speed, making it impossible for the pilot to close the distance, although the F-4 was flying at a speed greater than that of sound. The pilot and other crewmembers noted the great brilliance of the UFO, which, they said, appeared as a rectangular pattern of flashing coloured lights.

Suddenly, as the F-4 continued in its pursuit of the UFO, a smaller brilliant object, emerging from the UFO at high speed, headed directly for the pursuing F-4. The pilot was about to fire a missile at the approaching object, but his weapons-control panel went off, and he also lost all communications. The pilot turned and started to dive to avoid what he assumed was a projectile from the UFO. But the small object changed course, too, trailed the jet briefly, and then climbed back to rejoin the large UFO. The F-4 now renewed the chase. Suddenly, a second object left the side of the UFO; it dived at great speed towards the Earth and appeared to land gently in the hills far below. The large UFO now increased its speed to many times the speed of sound and disappeared. As they made long landing approach to the base, the F-4 crew noticed a cylindrical object about the size of a jet fighter approaching from a higher altitude. There were bright lights at each end of the object and a flashing light at its centre. The control tower personal knew of no other aircraft in the area, but confirmed the sighting visually. The incident was brought to the attention of the U.S. Defence Intelligence Agency, which considered it exceptionally important in the study of the UFOs.

95. Dreadful Warning

On May 3, 1975, Carlos Antonio de los Santos Montiel was flying to Mexico City, when his Piper PA-24 aircraft began shaking for no apparent reason. Moments later, the young pilot spotted a dark grey disk-shaped object, about 3 m in diameter, just beyond the plane's right wingtip. A similar craft was pacing him on the left. The most frightening of all, however, was a third object coming straight at him. The UFO passed just under his plane, so close, in fact, that it scraped the underpart of the fuselage.

De los Santos was nearly beside himself with fear. His terror was intensified when he discovered that the controls seemed frozen. He could not operate them yet, strangely, the plane continued flying at a steady speed of 190 km/h.

When the UFOs were no longer visible, De los Santos regained control of the plane. He instantly radioed the airport at Mexico City, and wept as he reported the incident.

The control tower took his report seriously, because the personnel there had tracked the objects on the radar. As air traffic controller, Emilio Estanol, told reporters, the objects made a 270-degree turn at 829 km/h in an arc of only 4.8 km. "Normally a plane moving at that speed needs 12 to 16 km to make a turn like that." He said, "In my seventeen years as an air traffic controller, I've never seen anything like that."

After De los Santos landed safely, he was given a medical examination, and pronounced fit. But as he would soon learn, his ordeal was not over. His sighting got headline treatment in the Mexican press and two weeks later, De los Santos, a retiring twenty-three-year-old man whose ambition in life was to become an airline pilot, was asked to appear on a television talk show to discuss his experience. He reluctantly agreed.

On the day, he was to appear, he drove his car down the free way on the way to the television station. Along the way he saw a large black automobile—he thought it looked like a diplomat's limousine—pull up in front of him. When he looked through the rear-view mirror, he saw an identical car behind him. The two cars, which looked so new that to all appearances they were being driven for the first time, were crowding him and soon forced him to the side of the road.

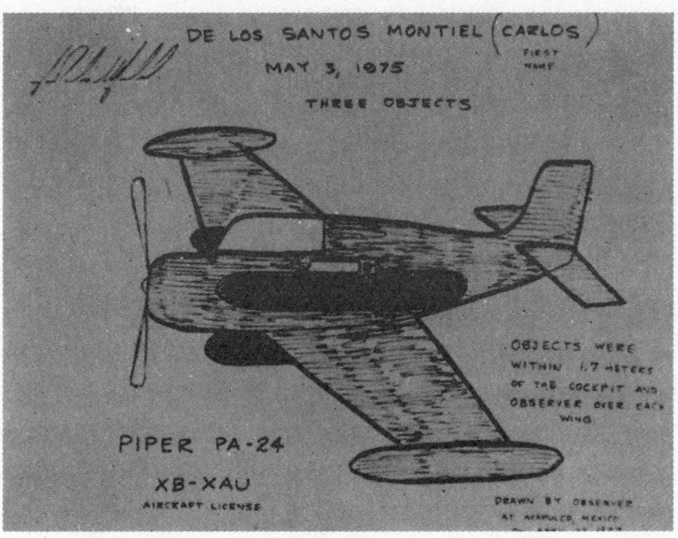

No sooner had he stopped than so did the other cars. De los Santos was about to get out when four tall, broad-shouldered men hopped out of their vehicles. One put his hand on Carlos's door as if to ensure that he would not be able to leave his car. He spoke quickly, speaking an oddly "mechanical" Spanish: "Look, boy if you value your life and your family's too, don't talk anymore about this sighting of yours."

De los Santos, too stunned to respond, watched the four

men, who were "Scandinavian" looking, with unusually pale skin and black suits, return to their cars and drove away. For his part, Carlos turned around and went back home.

Two days later, he told his story to Pedro Ferriz, the host of the television show on which he had been scheduled to appear. Ferriz, a UFO buff, said he had heard other reports of strange "men in black" who threatened the UFO witnesses. He assured the young pilot that despite the threats, he would not be hurt. In due course, he persuaded Carlos to do another interview, which went off without incident.

A month later, Carlos met Dr. J. Allen Hynek, the Northwestern University astronomer who had served as the U.S. Air Force's chief scientific consultant on UFO matters. The two talked and before they parted, Hynek invited him to have breakfast with him the next morning.

At 6:00 am, De los Santos left his house and went to the Mexicana Airlines office, where he had applied for a job. Then he went to Hynek's hotel.

As he walked up the steps, he was surprised to see one of the men in black, who had forced him off the freeway four weeks earlier. "You were already warned," the strange man said.

"You are not to talk about your experience." As if to underline the seriousness of the threat, he pushed Carlos back several metres.

"Look," he continued, "I don't want you to make problems for yourself. And why did you leave your house at six 0' clock this morning? Do you work for the Mexicana Airlines? Get out of here, and don't come back!"

De los Santo left immediately without meeting Hynek.

96. Disproportionately High Foreheads

At Ranton, near Sherwsbury, England, on October 11, 1954, at 4:45 pm, Mrs. Jennie Roestenberg and her two children watched a disk-shaped aluminum-coloured UFO hovering above their house. She claimed that she could see two "men" through two transparent panels on the side of the object. The occupants were very pale, had long, shoulder-length hair, and foreheads so disproportionately high that all the features seemed concentrated in the lower half of their faces. They wore turquoise-blue outfits resembling ski suits and transparent helmets. While the UFO was hovering at an angle, the two humanoids surveyed the scene "sternly, not in an unkindly fashion, but almost sadly, compassionately."

97. Torn into Pieces by Dogs

One of the most peculiar and tragic-close encounters ever reported occurred in May 1913, on a Farmersville, at a Texas farm, USA.

Three brothers, Silbie, Sid, and Clyde Latham, were chopping cotton when they heard their two dogs, Bob and Fox, barking, Silbie would recall, "just like they were in terrible distress." When the "deathly howl" continued, Clyde, the oldest, said, "Let's go up and see. Must be something pretty bad there."

The dogs were about 15 to 22 m away on the other side of a picket fence. Clyde, the first to get there, would be the first to see what had upset the dogs. "It's a little man!" he shouted.

According to Silbie Latham, who related the story to Larry Sessions of the Fort Worth Museum of Science and History, "He looked like he was resting on something. He was looking towards the north. He was no more than 45 cm high and dark green. He didn't have any clothes. Everything looked like a rubber suit, including the hat."

Right after the brothers arrived, Silbie said, the dogs jumped the entity and tore him to bits, leaving red blood and human looking internal organs on the grass.

"We were all just scared as hell and didn't know what to do about it," Silbie Latham would say to explain why he and his brothers had done nothing to stop the slaughter. "I guess we were just too dumb."

The boys went back to their chopping, occasionally returning to the spot to view the remains. The dogs huddled by them, as if afraid. The next day when the three returned to the site, there were no traces of any kind. All evidence of the little man was gone.

"My grandfather has a most solid reputation for truth and honesty but has never told this story outside the family for fear of ridicule," Lawrence Jones, Silbie Latham's grandson, recently told the Center of UFO Studies in Chicago.

"He has agreed to tell this only after much prompting and encouragement from me, his history-oriented grandson. He would take a polygraph or be hypnotised or whatever you need. There is no question in my mind that he is telling the truth."

98. South American UFO

On June 26, 1972 at 9:00 a.m. on this sunny winter day, farmer Bennie Smit was in his fields. One of his labourers, Boer de Klerk, ran up to tell him that he had seen a shiny spherical object with a bright 'star' atop it hovering over some nearby trees.

According to Boer de Klerk, the UFO was about a metre wide, and red when he first saw it, It moved among some bushes leaving a gray-white trail, and when it emerged it was green. Suddenly, it turned yellow-white. Smit got his 303 rifle and fired about eight shots at the UFO. The ball then slipped behind some trees, apparently unscathed. At about 10:00 a.m., two police officers arrived, and more shots were fired at the UFO, which was now black, but turned to gray. Smit hit the 'star', and the UFO stopped changing colour. Smit and the officers tried to approach the UFO, but it dodged away behind trees and bushes. Eventually, it disappeared into the impenetrable bush. Later, marks on the ground consistent with those made by a 'hard, heavy, spherical object' were found.

99. UFO Buster

The career of pioneer Freudian analyst Wilhelm Reich was so scarred with controversy that his most controversial work, his battle against invading the UFOs, was hardly noticed at all.

Born in Austria in 1897, Reich quickly displayed a temperamental genius for human psychology, becoming a Freudian convert while still at the university. In fact, he might have succeeded the master psychoanalyst had he not out-Freuded Freud, so to speak, with his insistence that free-flowing libido energy, otherwise known as the uninhibited orgasm, was an unmistakable sign of physical and mental health. That philosophy promptly got its author thrown out of the International Psychoanalytic Association as well as the fledgling Communist Party.

Reich became convinced that UFOs were interplanetary life form spying on his work, and also that they were accumulators of what he called "deadly orgone" that caused desertification of the planet. He wondered what would happen if he trained the hollow tubes of his cloudbuster on the UFOs. The answer came on the evening of October 10, 1954, as a series of red and yellow UFOs (beneficial ones, according to

Reich, would have been blue) converged over Orgonon. Reich declared that aiming the cloudbuster at the lights caused them to dim in intensity and take evasive action.

Writing in his logbook of the experiment, witnessed by several coworkers, Reich noted that, "Tonight for the first time in the history of man, the war waged from outer space upon this earth … was reciprocated … with positive result."

But Reich would not live to see the war won. He died in November 1957, while confined to a federal penitentiary for having refused to stop selling "orgone boxes," which he claimed could cure cancer.

100. UFO with a Sickening Stench

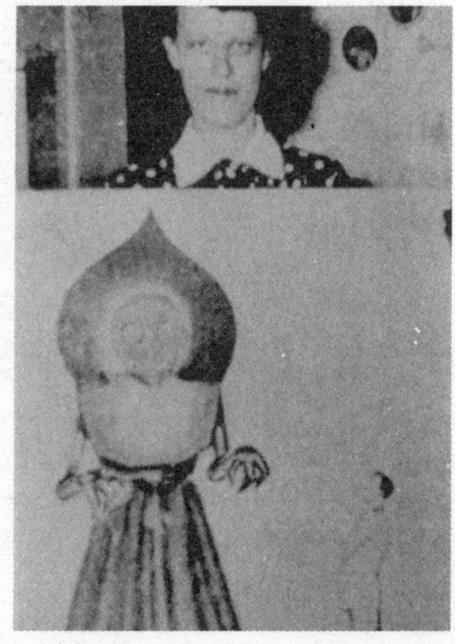

12 September 1952 - Flatwood, West Virginia, USA: Mrs Kathleen May, her five children and National Guardsman Gene Lemon, set out to investigate her sons' report that a UFO had landed on Flatwood Hill. The party reached the hill but fled in terror from a hooded monster 'worse than Frankenstein' - half man, half dragon, with a blood-red face and green eyes and 'terrible claws'.

A sickening stench came from the thing. Local people confirmed the landing of a sphere-shaped UFO on the hill, and the stench it left behind.

101. Four Linked UFOs

About an hour before sunset on December 8, 1981, Dan Luscomb watched a huge cigar-shaped object sail across the sky near Reserve, New Mexico. Luscomb, who owns the Whispering Pines Resort, 12 m south of Reserve, said the UFO was "as big as four 747s linked together." He also saw a jet pursue the strange object. "But everytime the plane got close," Luscomb recalls, "the object slipped away."

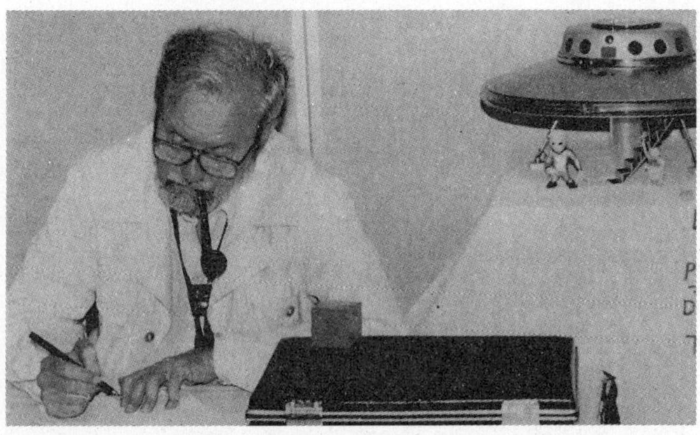

J. Allen Hynek, director of the Center for UFO Studies learned about Luscomb's sighting from an article in the *El Paso Times.* A few months later, in April, he decided to visit the Reserve to investigate the case personally.

Hynek found nine local people who insisted they, too, had seen the same cigar-shaped object at about the same time that Luscomb spotted it. Lance Swapp, an employee at Jake's Grocery Store in nearby Luna, said he saw a bright light while driving home from work. "When I got home, my brother was hollering at me to look up in the sky," he recalled. "There was a large object over our heads, with a jet on its trail."

Housewife Alma Hobbs reported she saw a red ball rising from the ground as she headed toward Luscomb's resort. A few seconds later, it turned sideways and she noted it was tubeshaped.

Hynek stated that whatever these witnesses saw, it wasn't a missile, which would have made deafening noise-the UFO over New Mexico was silent. He also concluded, "it was probably not a military test vehicle because no known technology can make a ninety-degree turn in seconds as this object allegedly did. The feat defies Newton's Second Law of Motion."

102. Farmer Gary T. Wilcox

On April 24, 1964, near Newark Village in Tioga County of New York State, sometime before 10:00 am, dairy farmer Gary T. Wilcox was spreading manure on a field near his farmhouse when he noticed something shiny about 720 m away. Among some trees at the top of the hill where he was working. He took it to be the wing tank or some other detached part of a damaged aircraft, and drove his tractor up the hill to investigate.

When Wilcox dismounted, he saw a cigar-shaped object about 6 m long and 5 m wide, hovering just off the ground. He kicked it. It felt like metallic canvas. Then, out from under it, came two 1.2 m tall creatures wearing seamless clothes and hoods over their heads that hid their features. Each was holding a tray of soil. In English, they said: "Do not be alarmed. We have talked to people before. We are from that you people refer to as the planet Mars." They then engaged Wilcox in a long conversation about fertilizers, explaining that they hoped to solve problems with "the rocky structure of Mars" by studying Earth's agricultural techniques. They also talked about space travel. They could come to Earth only every two years, and landed in daylight because their ship was less visible then. The two entities predicted the deaths of two Soviet cosmonauts and of US astronauts John Glenn and Virgil 'Gus' Grissom within the year. Finally, they asked for a bag of fertilizer. While Wilcox was walking to fetch it, the craft took off noiselessly and departed northwards at high speed. Later that day, Wilcox left a bag of fertilizer at the landing site. Next morning, it had gone.

103. The Abduction of Charles Hickson and Calvin Parker

On October 11, 1973, Charles E. Hickson, aged 45, and Calvin R. Parker Jr. aged, 19, were spending the evening fishing off the pier of the abandoned Shaupeter shipyard on the Pascagoula River. At about 9:00 pm, Hickson turned to get a fresh bait, and heard a 'zipping sound'.

Hickson saw an egg-shaped blue-gray craft hovering close to the ground nearby. An opening appeared in the UFO and three 1.5 m creatures floated out of it. Each had gray, wrinkled skin, pincers for hands, small cone-shaped ears and a small pointed nose. The entities gathered up the two fishermen - at this point, Parker fainted - and floated them into the craft. Hickson then found himself in a brightly-lit room with no visible light source. Parker was taken to an adjoining chamber.

Hickson was suspended so that he could move only his eyes, and a free-floating object resembling a gigantic eye moved back and forth above his body, as if examining it. After 20 minutes or so, the pair were floated back to the pier. Hickson landed on his feet. Parker then regained consciousness. The UFO was gone 'in less than a second'.

104. Crop Circles

In 1965, there were two UFO sightings at a point called Colloway Clump on the Warminster-Westbury Road in Wiltshire. And in a field near the bend in the road, circular depressions were found in the crops, which were labelled as 'UFO nests'.

In the 1980s, a Wiltshire farmer named John Scull found his oats crushed to the ground in three separate circles not far from Colloway Clump. The circles were surrounded by undamaged oats and no path through the corn suggested intruders.

As the decade progressed, there were an increasing numbers of these 'crop circles'. Many of these reports come from southern England, but there are others from Australia, New Zealand, Argentina, Brazil, South Africa, Mexico, America, Canada, France, Spain, Switzerland, Austria, Germany, Sweden, Russia and even Japan. In many cases, the crop circles were found in fields near UFO sightings.

Scientific investigators suggest that the circles were created by some kind of natural whirlwind, at which point, circles began to appear in more complex forms – sometimes like a Celtic cross. Another crop patterns seemed to represent a kind of chemical retort with a long neck, with four rectangles neatly spaced on either side of it.

Witnesses came forward who had seen the grass laid out flat as a curious humming sound vibrated through the air. One witness who rushed forward into the circle said that he seemed to be caught up in a whirlwind. A moment later, everything was still.

In 1990, John Michell made the suggestion that the meaning of the crop circles "is to be found in the way people are affected by them".

He seemed to feel that crop circles could be some kind of a 'teaching experience' designed to awaken people's minds to wider possibilities.

In 1991, two men called Douglas Bower and David Chorley admitted that since 1978, they had faked hundreds of crop circles in the south of England, and demonstrated how they did it using wooden boards and lengths of twine. But they never claimed to have made any of the earlier crop circles, and investigators pointed out that, as in an earlier hoax perpetrated by the *Daily Mirror*, the Chorley-Bower crop circles were visibly amateurish.

105. Was it Really a Helium Balloon?

Delta Airlines flight 1083 departed Pittsburgh on June 15, 1987. It was bound for Atlanta. However, enroute, the passenger plane was flying over West Virginia when the pilot sighted an object heading towards the craft. The 1.2 m, finned "missile," he told the *St. Louis Post-Dispatch*, was travelling with great speed and narrowly missed the plane, as it passed slightly below it and to the side.

The defence department denied ownership of the so-called missile, and the National Weather Service claimed it was probably not one of its instruments. At the New York regional headquarters of the Federal Aviation Administration (FAA), the spokesperson, Kathleen Bergen, proposed that it might have been a blimp-shaped helium balloon. The weather service, however, countered that the wind in the jet stream over West Virginia at the time was too weak to make a balloon move as swiftly as the pilot said the object had.

Nevertheless, the FAA's official position was that the object was an escaped promotion balloon. "Balloons can travel pretty far," Bergen explained, adding, "We don't acknowledge the existence of UFOs."

106. Celebrity Sightings

One film star, who has seen a UFO, is German-born actress, Elke Sommer. In 1978, she was in the garden of her Los Angeles home when a shiny orange ball, about 6m in diameter, appeared out of blue. "It came glowing and floating about like a big moon," she said. "It came towards me and I fled into the house. When I reappeared, it had vanished."

Boxer Muhammad Ali was on a training session in New York's Central Park in 1972 when he encountered a UFO. He said: "I was out jogging just before sunrise, when this bright light hovered over me. It just seemed to be watching me. It was like a huge electric light bulb in the sky."

Statesmen and politicians, who have seen UFOs, include John Gilligan, governor of Ohio, who, in 1973, was reported to have seen a UFO near Ann Arbor, Michigan. He described it as 'a vertical shaft of light which glowed amber'.

Sir Eric Gairey, prime minister of the Caribbean island of Grenada, tried unsuccessfully in 1978 to have the United Nations officially investigate UFOs. He said he himself had seen one – "a brilliant golden light travelling at tremendous speed".

107. Fifteen More Calls That Night

The following statement was made by Pedro Saucedo and confirmed by a fellow driver, who was with him on a Texas highway on the night of November 2, 1957:

"I was driving my truck on route 116, going north, 6.5 km out of Levelland (Texas). I saw a big flame ahead.... I thought it was a lightning, but when this object had reached my position it was different, because it put my truckmotor and the lights out.... It looked like a torpedo, about 60 m long, moving at the speed of about 950 to 1280 km/h.

When the blazing lights of the UFO vanished into the distance, the truck's headlights came on again, and the engine started up easily.

Patrolman A. J. Fowler, who received the initial, and somewhat hysterical phone call from Saucedo, who was reporting the incident, recorded 15 more calls that night from persons who had seen some kind of a large UFO at the same time their car engines had died out. According to the signed statement made later by one of the callers:

"I ... noticed an oval-shaped object-flat on the bottom-sitting on the road ahead ... about 38 m long ... glowing with a bluish-green light. The object seemed to be made of an aluminum-like material, but had no markings. The object finally rose into the air, almost straight up."

108. Risks of Washing Day

A terrified Devon housewife claimed she was grabbed by aliens, and beamed onto a spaceship, as she pegged washing out in her back garden in February 1978.

The woman, who asked to remain anonymous when quizzed by UFO researchers, said she first saw a blue shining shape approach her home in Ermington, near Plymouth, from the north.

"The light hovered over the garden," she said. "I was petrified. I dropped the washing. Suddenly, I was completely enveloped in bubbles of light. I saw three beings, who looked like men. They did not speak. They were about five- feet tall, wearing bluish metallic-like clothing."

They grasped me by the arms, and we were lifted up to a beam of light into a kind of room. There were more of the men there. I was given the impression – I don't know how – that I would come to no harm.

"A little later, I found myself back on my lawn. I felt a sharp blow on the back of my neck. I was stunned but not hurt. When I looked around, the thing set off at great speed and disappeared."

The woman, identified only as Mrs G, told her strange story to Contact UK, one of the largest British UFO investigating organisations. Bernard Delair, one of its senior members, said: "We take this report very seriously. Her story is very graphic and fits many others."

109. Tunguska Incident

On June 30, 1908 at seven o'clock in the morning, an enormous explosion was heard from the isolated forests of Siberia, particularly the Tunguska region.

Subsequent investigation revealed that there had been a number of hunters and fishermen in the area who had seen an object travelling through the sky. It was described as more brilliant than the sun and heading towards the site of the explosion.

The impact was so great that even 800 km away, one train driver stopped his train in the belief that his own cargo had exploded. There were shock waves over a great distance, and the event was recorded all around the world, including London, England.

In the 1920s, an expedition to the region discovered that there had apparently been something like an airborne explosion, rather than the meteorite impact that the team had expected to find. The debris in the forest was very similar to the debris at Hiroshima following the airborne explosion of an atomic bomb in 1945.

In other words, there was total devastation radiating out from one central point, but at the point of 'ground zero', the destroyed trees were still standing, while the others radiating out from that central point were felled.

A meteorite would not have caused such devastation. Of course, in 1908 there could not have been atomic blasts, leaving the speculation that the Tunguska explosion was due to an extraterrestrial nuclear-powered craft exploding in the air.

However, there may be other more natural explanations, which have not yet been fully understood by science, i.e., some particularly destructive form of ball lightning or plasma energy.

110. A Great Breakthrough

In September 1977, at Phoenix, Arizona, a UFO group filed a lawsuit against the CIA under the Freedom of Information Act. William Spaulding, Director of Ground Saucer Watch Incorporation, alleged that the agency possessed thousands of documents about its involvement with the UFOs, and had actively conspired to keep them secret from the public by denying their existence.

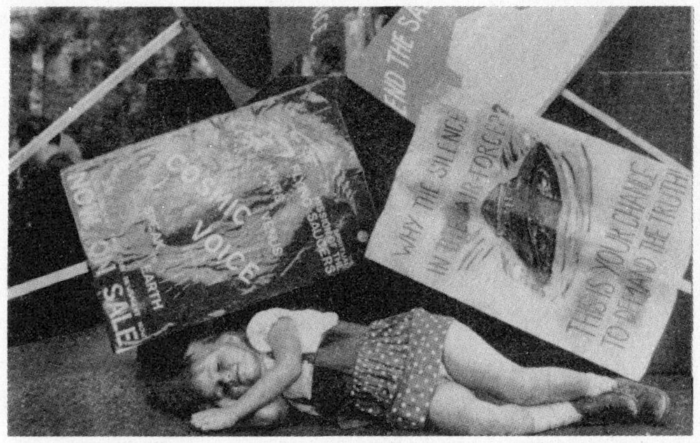

The case was backed by Citizens Against UFO Secrecy, a national body, and the CIA lost it. A Washington judge ordered them to search their files for all the UFO material.

A total of 10,000 pages were found, but only 900 released, the rest being withheld on national security grounds. Nevertheless, Citizens Against the UFO Secrecy hailed it as a victory. Even the admission that files existed was a breakthrough against the blanket of governmental obfuscation.

111. UFO-Caused Car Accidents

In the summer of 1979, two teenaged boys watched unexplained lights pass over their car. Then some sort of energy pinned them to their seats. When the youngsters were finally able to drive away, they found their car racing out of control, as if it had a mind of its own.

A couple of weeks later, at 1:40 a.m, a Minnesota policeman saw an unusual light in the sky and felt his car being blown across the road by an unseen force. Then he blacked out. When he came to his senses, the officer found that his windshield had been shattered and his antenna bent. His clock was inexplicably fourteen minutes slow.

According to the Centre for UFO Studies in Evanston, Illinois, these incidents are not unique. There have been 440 cases reported around the world of the UFOs provoking car accidents or near accidents. The UFOs appear to initiate "electro-chemical events" that can stall engines and break or block radios with a static force.

Most of the incidents have no scientific explanation, says astrophysicist, Mark Rodeghier, who has studied reports. He points out that the Ford LTD driven by the Minnesota policeman was examined by Ford engineers, who insisted that no known phenomenon could cause the automobile to behave in such a strange way.

112. The Work of the Devil

The Church frowns on the growing interest in unidentified flying objects. The Bishop of Norwich, one of the two top clerics who attended the 1979 House of Lords debate on the subject, said: "I am very concerned. The mystery surrounding

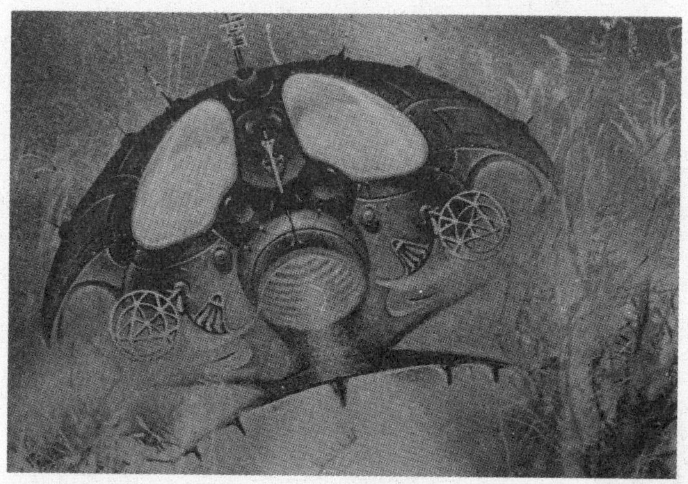

the UFOs today is helping to build up a climate of credulity, and, in certain cases, even of superstition, with the danger of ersatz spirituality."

One clergyman, who has studied the UFOs for 30 years and written a book about them, believes they are the work of the Devil, and have an evil influence on people. Rev Eric Inglesby said: "People expect the UFOs to be benevolent beings. There is no proof whatsoever that this is the case. Quite the opposite, I have known many cases where people have been very disturbed, even to the point of a form of spirit possession, which in many cases is undoubtedly evil. Some of the UFOs are frightfully dangerous. I even know cases where people were so oppressed by sightings of the UFOs that they had to be exorcized by a priest."

113. Without Any Question

On December 31, 1978 an Argosy cargo plane, carrying a three- member Melbourne television crew, headed by Channel O reporter, Quentin Fogorty, was retracing the flight path between Wellington and Christchurch, a route along which bright, unidentified lights had been observed by aircraft crews for several weeks.

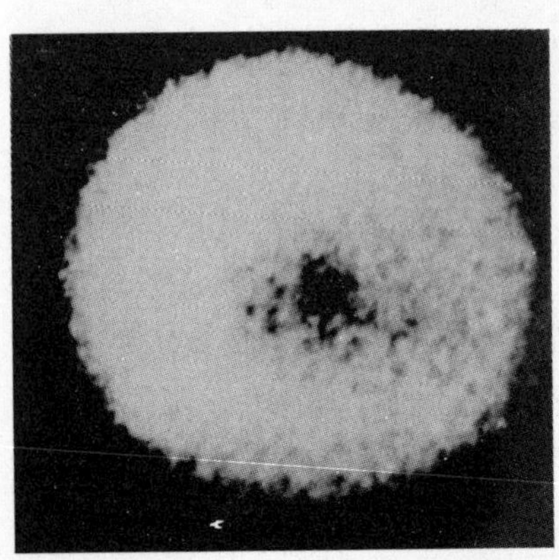

On the flight down, the evening of December 30, the team saw some mysterious lights that moved too erratically to catch on the film. But the flight back from Christchurch to Blenheim was more rewarding. At 2:15 a.m, something approached within 16 km of the cargo plane. One of the TV crew described it as having a "brightly lit base and a sort of transparent dome." The object was picked up by the craft's radar. What was most exciting was successfully photographed on 16 mm colour film. The UFO maintained a certain distance from the plane for a time, then it moved to the front, to the left, and finally sped away. Ground radar confirmed unidentified blips near the plane at the time.

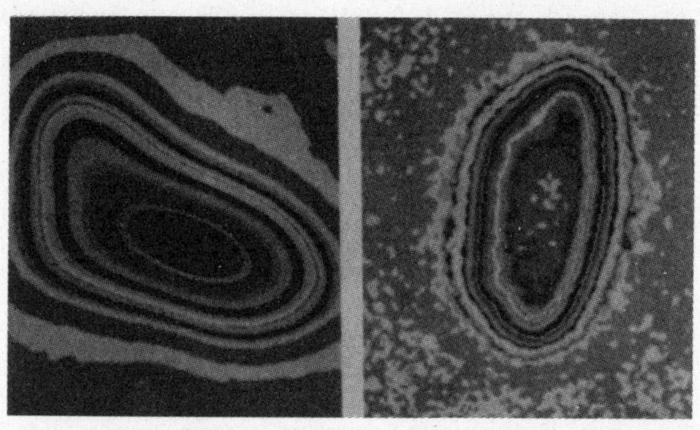

Some 23,000 frames of film were turned over for analysis to Dr. Bruce Maccabee, an optical physicist employed by the U.S. Navy. The film showed several brief sequences of strange, unidentifiable images, one of which had the bell-shaped form mentioned by the cameraman. Another frame showed the track of the UFO as it described a figure-eight loop. Still another sequence showed an object changing from a large, bright, yellowish round shape to a dim, more reddish, triangular shape. Dr. Maccabee estimated that one of the objects was 18 to 30 metres in diameter and emitted a light equivalent to the candlepower of a 100,000-watt bulb. The UFO executing the loop was estimated to be travelling at the speed of roughly 4,800 km/h.

The film and other documentations were later submitted to a score of U.S. scientists, experts in optics, biophysics, radar, optical physiology and astronomy.

Despite several previous official statements rejecting the observations as a natural phenomena, this team unanimously agreed that the recorded lights were not explicable in terms of Venus or other planets, stars, meteors, high-altitude balloons, off-course aircraft, satellites, atmospheric illusions, reflected lights, or even a hoax. The things seen, filmed and trailed by the radar between Christchurch and Blenheim were without question unidentifiable flying objects.

114. Underground Facilities for Defence

The Hollywood Blockbuster movie, *Independence Day*, features a sequence supposed to take place in the top secret underground military facility known as "Area 51". The UFO folklore has it

that this installation contains all recovered remains of an alien and their craft that the US government wants to investigate in secret. Although there is absolutely no hard evidence that the base exists, it is known that the US government does have many secret underground facilities.

In 1987, Lloyed A. Duscha, a senior officer in the US Army Engineer Corps, gave a speech entitled, "Underground Facilities for Defence: Experience and Lessons" at a conference on subterranean construction. He spoke for sometime about the general theory employed by the army, using as example the well-known nuclear defence installations. He went on, "........there are projects of similar scope, which I cannot identify, but which include multiple chambers of up to 15 m wide and 30 m high using the same excavation procedures.........."

References

1. Brooksmith, Peter – *UFO, The Complete Sighting Catalogue,* 1995
2. Blunder, Nigel and Boar, Roger – *The World's Greatest UFO Mysteries,* 1983
3. Sachs, Margaret and John Ernest – *Celestial Passengers, UFOs & Space Travel,* 1978
4. Randels, Jenny – *Paranormal Source Book,* 1999
5. Berlitz, Charles – *World of Odd and the Awesome,* 1991
6. Spencer, John – *The UFO Encyclopaedia,* 1999
7. Cawthorne, Nigel – *The World's Greatest Abductions,* 2000
8. Berlitz, Charles and Moore L. William – *Roswell Incident,* 1988
9. Colin, Wilson – *World Famous UFOs,* Parragon
10. Cawthorne, Nigel – *The World's Greatest Alien Encounters,* 2002
11. Wilson, Rowan – *UFOs, Amazing Stories of the Unexplained,* 1997
12. Matthews, Rupert – *UFOs and Aliens,* 1988

13. Barclay, David and Barclay, Therese Marie – *UFOs, The Final Answer,* 1993

14. Berlitz, Charles – *World of Strange Phenomena,* 1988

15. Johannes von Buttlar – *The UFO Phenomenon,* 1979

16. Alien Books – *Aliens,* 1996

17. Schnabel, Jim – *Dark White,* 1994

18. Octopus Publishing Group – *The World's Greatest UFO and Alien Encounters,* 2002

19. Alien Books – *The UFO Files,* 1996

20. Colin, Wilson – *Alien Dawn,* 1998

21. Asimov, Issac – *Extraterrestrial Civilisations,* 1980

22. Adamski, George – *Flying Saucers Have Landed,* 1953

23. Bryan, C.D.B. – *Close Encounter of the Fourth Kind,* 1995

24. Chariton, Wallace O. – *The Great Texas Airship Mystery,* 1990

25. Wilkins, Harold T. – *Flying Saucers on Attack,* 1954

26. Walton, Travis – *Fire in the Sky,* 1990

27. Trench, Brinsley and Le Poer – *The Sky People,* 1960

28. Shuttlewood, Arthur – *The Flying Saucers,* 1976

29. Good, Timothy – *Beyond Top Secret,* 1996

30. Ford, Brian – *The Earth Watchers,* 1973

31. David, Jay – *The Flying Saucer Reader,* 1967

32. Keel, John A. – *Our Haunted Planet,* 1971

33. Hopkins, Budd – *Witnessed,* 1996

34. Holzer, Hans – *The Ufonauts,* 1976

35. Blum, Ralph and Judy – *Beyond Earth : Man's Contact with UFOs,* 1974

36. Striber, Whitley – *Communion,* 1987

37. Klass, Philip – *UFO Abductions : A Dangerous Game,* 1988

38. Evans, Hilary – *Visions, Apparitions and Alien Visitors,* 1984

39. Brown, Charles (ed.) – *The Humanoids,* 1974

40. Johannes von Buttlar – *Time Slip,* 1979

41. Fry, Daniel – *The White Sands Incidents,* 1966

42. Hobana, Ion – *UFO from Behind the Iron Curtain,* 1975

43. Barker, Gray – *America's Captured Flying Saucers – Cover Up of the Century,* 1977

44. Chatelin, Maurice – *Our Ancestors Came from Outer Space,* 1977

45. Davidson, Dr. Leoan, Ed. *Flying Saucers, An Analysis of Air Force Project Blue Book Special Report No. 14.,* 1971

46. Faucher, Eric; Goodstein, Ellen; and Gris Henry – *Alien UFOs Watched Our First Astronauts on the Moon,* 1979

47. Huyghe, Patrick – *UFO Files : The Untold Story,* 1979

48. Stringfield, Leonard H. – *Retrieval of the Third Kind, MUFON UFO Journal,* 1978

49. *Time* (January 9, 1950) p. 49 – *Visitors from Venus*

50. *Time* (March 1, 1954) p. 12-13 – *The Presidency*

51. *U.S. News & World Report* (February 26, 1954) p.6 – *People of the week – Dwight Eisenhower*

52. Hynek, Dr. J. Allen – *Hynek UFO Report,* 1978

53. Basterfield – *Close Encounters of an Australian Kind,* 1981

54. Cassierer, Manfred – *Parapsychology and the UFO,* 1988

55. Walter, Ed and Walter, Francis – *UFO Abductions in Gulf Breeze,* 1994

56. Kinder, Gary – *Light Years,* 1987

57. Dong, Paul – *The Four Major Mysteries of Mainland China,* 1984

58. Khatri, Vikas – *Mysteries around UFOs* (Hindi), 2002

By the Same Author

Endangered Animals of the World

For the first time, a well-illustrated collection of over 100 threatened animals

This rare book turns spotlight on world's endangered animals, and captures them in their natural splendour. It gives an in-depth analysis of many threatened species, such as, Polar bear, Black buck, Giant panda, Black rhinoceros, Brazilian tapir, platypus etc, living on this planet.

Packed with information and based on the observation of leading naturalists, the book discusses threadbare these animals' habitat, scientific name, family, food and area of location. It enlightens the readers about the preservation of these species and creates awareness about their role for the harmonious sustenance of the mother planet.

Lavishly peppered with illustrations, it will leave you hungry for more.

Pages: 160

Price: Rs. 100/- Postage: Rs. 15/-

By the Same Author

Dreams & Premonitions

Some dreams and premonitions are prophetic. They came true in the life of many eminent world personalities like Julius Caesar, Abraham Lincoln, Adolf Hitler, Mark Twain, H.G.Wells and John Lenon foretelling death, calamities and disasters with pin-point accuracy. Thus, to discount them as being coincidental is not only preposterous, but also to defy divinity.

The present book turns spotlight on a wide range of dreams and extra-sensory perceptions covering wars, crimes, discoveries, science and murders. Mind boggling, thrilling, startling yet time proven !!!

Pages: 152 • Price: Rs. 100/- Postage: Rs. 15/-

True Ghosts & Spooky Incidents

Haunted castles, headless apparitions, psychic experiences and invisible moanings—if these fascinate you, then read on. This book, as the title suggests, is a spell-binding, spine-chilling compilation of ghostly, out-of-this-world appearances. Be it the middle of an ocean, a secluded castle in the mountains or a sentried jailhouse, ghosts—both friendly and evil—have managed to gain entry to the most improbable places and scared the wits out of hapless multitudes.

Believe them or not, The Mummy that sank the Titanic, A Phone-call from the Dead, The Restless Skull and other spectral beings will keep you glued to the book.

There is no guarantee that you won't suffer nightmares, but we do hope you will keep your mind open and enjoy these spooky, thrilling stories as they are—true and creepy !!!

Pages: 136 • Price: Rs. 100/- Postage: Rs. 15/-